At David C Cook, we equip the local church around
the corner and around the globe to make disciples.
Come see how we are working together—go to
www.davidccook.org. Thank you!

DAVID **C** COOK

transforming lives together

What people are saying about …

HERE I AM

'It's hard to fathom just how many lives will have been touched in some way by the gospel of Jesus Christ through the reaching-out of The Message. And who can tell what lies ahead? Being around this ministry, you can't help but think that the best is still yet to come.'

Matt Redman, songwriter and worship leader

'Andy is a man possessed with the living spirit of prophetic fiery imagination. He can literally see the world made new. What I love most about Andy is in the pages of this book. He is not content to think great thoughts or have wonderful redemptive theology, or even rest on the exploits he has already done. Andy has a fresh vision for today, and it's full of fire. This man has invested his entire life to the redemption of the world and is about to increase the pace. For those of us who are amazed just watching him, he remains a living inspiration and invitation to get on with the work Jesus started. God's kingdom come!'

Danielle Strickland, speaker, advocate, and author

'I vividly remember Andy's role in Festival: Manchester in 2003. Andy and I worked closely to cast the vision of the festival, unite the

Church around evangelism, and proclaim the good news boldly. At the launch of the festival—after a rich time of worship and prayer—I remember Andy saying to the crowd: "Did you feel Manchester tremble?" I was stirred by the comment, and it has stuck with me all these years. It seemed to clearly express Andy's vision, passion, and enthusiasm, as well as his deep sensitivity to the things of God.

'From the moment I first met him, I knew the hand of God was on his life. His love for people and his exuberance for spreading the good news of Jesus were deeply touching. Through his leadership and God's guidance, The Message Trust has become a powerful force in the United Kingdom. Their ministry has helped reveal the love of God and His compassion to hundreds of thousands of hurting and broken people. More than twenty-five years have gone by, and the joy and vision are still increasing. Personally, I rejoice at what the future looks like for The Message Trust and its godly team members.'

Luis Palau, world evangelist and author

JOINING GOD'S
ADVENTUROUS
CALL TO LOVE
THE WORLD

HERE
I AM

ANDY HAWTHORNE

DAVID C COOK

transforming lives together

HERE I AM
Published by David C Cook
4050 Lee Vance Drive
Colorado Springs, CO 80918 U.S.A.

Integrity Music Limited, a Division of David C Cook
Eastbourne, East Sussex BN23 6NT, England

The graphic circle C logo is a registered trademark of David C Cook.

The website addresses recommended throughout this book are offered as a
resource to you. These websites are not intended in any way to be or imply an
endorsement on the part of David C Cook, nor do we vouch for their content.

Details in some stories have been changed to protect
the identities of the persons involved.

Unless otherwise noted, all Scripture quotations are taken from Holy Bible, New
International Version® Anglicised, NIV® Copyright © 1979, 2011 by Biblica,
Inc.® Used by permission. All rights reserved worldwide. Scripture quotations
marked NLT are taken from the *Holy Bible*, New Living Translation, copyright ©
1996, 2004, 2015 by Tyndale House Foundation. Used by permission of Tyndale
House Publishers, Inc., Carol Stream, Illinois 60188. All rights reserved.

LCCN 2018909357
ISBN 978-0-8307-7653-5
eISBN 978-0-8307-7654-2

The Team: Ian Matthews, Jeff Gerke, Jennie Pollock,
Amy Konyndyk, Nick Lee, Susan Murdock
Cover Design: Mark Prentice at beatroot.media
Cover Image: © TheStockCube / Adobe Stock

Printed in the United Kingdom
First Edition 2019

1 2 3 4 5 6 7 8 9 10

112118

*To Michele—my partner in life, love,
and ministry for nearly forty years*

CONTENTS

FOREWORD

These three words, "Here I am", describe Andy Hawthorne's life and message perfectly. It was more than thirty years ago that he first said, "Here I am. Send me!" and he's still saying it today. The results of this simple act of obedience have been incredible. Countless lives have been changed, broken hearts have been mended, eternal destinies have been rewritten. Andy's home city of Manchester (and many other places too) would be profoundly different if he had not said "Here I am" all those years ago. In this brilliant resource, written out of decades of hard-won experience, Andy shares the insights that will challenge you to respond in the same way.

One of the many things I like about Andy is that he's never pretended to be perfect. But then again, neither did the prophet Isaiah, who first spoke these words thousands of years ago. He said, "Woe to me! I am ruined! For I am a man of unclean lips, and I live among a people of unclean lips, and my eyes have seen the King!" Don't write yourself off because you think you're too broken, or too bad, or too boring. God is calling you, and this book will help you respond.

Some people think it's a scary thing, a brave thing, and a miserable thing to respond to God's call. But they're flat-out wrong. The stupidest, most dangerous thing you can ever do is to say no to the One who knows you best, loves you best, and only wants the best for your life. The safest, most sensible, and most exciting thing you can ever do (and okay, I admit that it can be a bit scary too) is to stand before God—whose heart is breaking for the world—and say: "Here I am."

Pete Greig
Emmaus Rd, Guildford and 24-7 Prayer International

ACKNOWLEDGEMENTS

Here I Am has been very much a team effort, but special thanks must go to Ian Matthews from David C Cook UK for managing the whole project and Jeff Gerke from David C Cook USA for great work on the manuscript.

Thanks also to Al Metcalfe, Simon Baker, David Hailes, and The Message's creative team for their support and work on the accompanying videos, and as ever, many thanks to Danielle Campsall for keeping the show on the road.

INTRODUCTION

"Here I am! Send me!"

It's one of the most famous lines in the Bible. The prophet Isaiah had just encountered the Most High God, and within the span of only a few moments, he had been transformed from cowering before the holiness of God because he was "a man of unclean lips" into a volunteer jumping up and down with his arm raised high, begging for the honour of being sent out to do his Lord's will.

Like Isaiah, so many of God's children long to serve in His epic work and yet don't know how to begin or what that might look like. We sense that the Lord Jesus may be calling us into action, and we know there is much in the world that needs His touch, and yet we don't know how to proceed. He's engaged in an adventurous campaign to love the world, and we're willing volunteers, but we don't know where to turn or what to do first.

And, frankly, there may still be an element of counting the cost. If we give ourselves fully to the Lord's call, what will be asked of us? We may feel a desire to reach the lost, the least, and the last but have no idea how to proceed—or whether we'll be obliged to leave our home and enter the jungles of Africa. We may have deep compassion for the poor and marginalised but be secretly concerned that God might ask us to give away all our possessions. The urban centres of our cities need the light of Jesus, but what could happen to us or our kids if we went there?

It's not that we're thinking about lowering our hand. We're not having second thoughts about crying, "Here I am—send me!" It's simply that we're wishing for some clarification about the path and, honestly, the courage to go ahead and jump.

I applaud you, fellow volunteer! You have heard the voice of the Most High and you have raised your hand to be sent! How many are called, and yet how few step forward or even explore what the call might entail?

I started where you are. Indeed, every man or woman of God who has ever been used to do some good in the world started out where you are. Willing and eager but in need of guidance.

In the pages of this book, I hope you are going to find what you're seeking. I'm going to help you understand your calling, your journey to preparedness, the heart of God Himself, and your place in His good work to love the people of this world.

THAT'S HOW IT WAS WITH ME

As I write this, I'm aware that you may know about me already or you may not. If you've heard my name, it might be in relation to the 1990s British Christian dance band World Wide Message Tribe (later named The Tribe). The band had success in the UK and America. Or you may have heard of me as the founder of The Message Trust, a mission organisation based in Manchester, England.

But what's perhaps most significant about me is that I had my own "Whom shall I send?" invitation from God, and I answered it. It resulted in the formation of a ministry that has been working for thirty years to improve the lives of young people in the UK and beyond through our work in schools, prisons, and communities.

My "Whom shall I send?" moment came in 1987, when my brother, Simon, and I received a vision to hold the biggest youth mission that Manchester had ever seen. Our dream was to book the city's biggest rock venue, the Apollo, for a week and fill it with the best Christian bands, theatre companies, and evangelists we could get our hands on. We wanted to partner with the local church on hundreds of local missions, with a special focus on the hardest to reach. It was ambitious, naïve, and likely to fail, but it was our attempt to answer the calling of God.

If you don't live in the United Kingdom, you may not be aware of the spiritual condition here. In 1955, over fifty percent of British citizens went to church, and roughly the same percentage of church-attenders were in their twenties. By 2005, that number had gone down to well under ten percent of the whole population—with just three percent of British church attenders being in their 20s. In 2014 the former Archbishop of Canterbury, Rowan Williams, declared England "a post-Christian nation."

When Simon and I were attempting to put this massive event together, we often returned home at the end of the day feeling defeated and discouraged. How were two guys in their mid-twenties, with no connections and not a lot of money, going to pull this vision off? We must have heard it wrong from God!

But then, as has happened many times in my life, Isaiah came to the rescue.

Sitting in my room, alone on my bed, I despondently picked up my Bible to do the set reading for the day. My prayer was simple: "God, if this vision is from You, please speak to me from Your Word." Here was the reading that had been selected for the day:

> Forget the former things;
>> do not dwell on the past.
> See, I am doing a new thing!
>> Now it springs up; do you not perceive it?
> I am making a way in the wilderness
>> and streams in the wasteland.
> The wild animals honour me,
>> the jackals and the owls,
> because I provide water in the wilderness
>> and streams in the wasteland,

to give drink to my people, my chosen,

the people I formed for myself

that they may proclaim my praise. (Isaiah

43:18–21)

The words landed joyfully in my heart. I knew God was speaking directly to us. I phoned Simon straight away and told him, "God is going to do this!"

We put those verses on the bottom of our first letterhead, and we used them when we wrote to every church in Manchester.

God *was* doing a new thing then. The Manchester outreach, called Message '88, attracted around 20,000 young people. They heard live performances by bands and a bold presentation of the gospel message. The next year we did it all again. Out of Message '89, Simon and I were approached by a band member and challenged to form an organisation that would go into Manchester schools with hip-hop and dance music—and the gospel.

The Message arose out of those efforts, and now, thirty years on, we have active urban ministries throughout England and in Scotland, Wales, Canada, and South Africa, and we have contact with hundreds of thousands of young people every year.

God continues His work. And that same passage from Isaiah is the first thing you see hanging from the walls when you enter our headquarters. God's gifts and calling are irrevocable (Romans 11:29). The things He wanted His people to do then are the same things He wants His people to do now. Isaiah called God's people to justice, mercy, and release of the oppressed, and these are the very things Jesus calls Christians to today.

Keep that in mind, my friend. Whatever God is calling you to do will be found within that same mission.

At The Message, our focus is on extending God's invitation for salvation and rescue in the toughest, most financially deprived neighbourhoods of cities across the UK and the world. God might be calling you to join us, or He might have another area of mission in which you should operate.

A NEW THING PEOPLE

Let's take a closer look at this passage, as it shaped what The Message became. This passage describes what I believe God wants for every church, ministry, or *person* who wants to change the world.

First, you and I need to be "See, I am doing a new thing" people (see verse 19). God is always creative, and He's always got new things for His people to do to bless the world. It's called being pioneering and apostolic. When you are this way, you open up new good spaces for others to enter into, as well.

Second, you and I need to embrace that we are "Do you not perceive it?" people (see verse 19 again). No matter how carefully we keep our eyes open for the new things the Lord is doing, we can't possibly see it all with the unaided gaze. God must provide the perception so that we may see what He's up to. But we can pursue God's perception by seeking the Lord through prayer and fasting. There has never been a major move of God in history that didn't have a corps of believers seeking insight into His will for the world.

Third, you and I must be "Wild animals honour me" people (verse 20). We must believe that the wild animals of our world—people whom society considers the biggest problems—have deep value to God and can actually be part of the world's biggest solution. Every bit of evidence down through history points to the fact that, if there's going to be a major move of God, it will almost certainly start on the margins.

Fourth, you and I need to be "Streams in the wasteland" (or "Rivers in the desert") people (verse 20). You and I need to believe that God wants to send a flood of life into the hardest places. I remember seeing a video of rainwater arriving in a dry valley in the Negev Desert in Israel—the very desert that Isaiah prophesied about. Things don't grow there until there's rain in the mountains. When people see rain falling in the mountains, they get excited. They know that life is going to come flowing down to them soon. They know that rivers are going to flow and that everyone's going to have water to drink and that things will begin growing.

The video I saw was of one such event. The people had seen rain falling on the mountains, and so they'd gathered to witness the moment when the rain arrived from the mountains and rushed into the valley, flooding everything in its path. When I saw it, my spirit jumped. You and I must believe that God wants to, and will, send life-giving water flowing down from the mountain of God into the thirsty lives of those who do not know Him. God is a "Rivers in the desert" God, and we must be "Rivers in the desert" people.

When we adopt these four aspects of God's intent, we cultivate our hearts to be fertile ground for God's calling. As you consider what God might be calling you into, run it through these four points and let them refine your expectations.

When we applied these things to The Message, we realised we needed to develop a multi-level strategy involving music bands and theatre companies who boldly proclaim the gospel, and dozens of Eden teams—teams of volunteers who choose to live long-term in the most deprived communities and enterprise centres, providing jobs, homes, and intensive support for the most vulnerable people who have come to Christ.

I don't know how these four elements will figure in your calling. But I can say without question that exploring them will help you find your part in the great adventure God has for you.

With this in mind, we can turn to the primary passage of Scripture, also from Isaiah, that will guide our entire discussion in this book. Because one thing remains clear: God is still asking, "Whom shall I send?"

OUR CORE PASSAGE

Here I Am is organised around a famous passage in Isaiah, in which God calls the prophet into His service. Here is that passage:

> In the year that King Uzziah died, I saw the Lord,
> high and exalted, seated on a throne; and the train

of his robe filled the temple. Above him were seraphim, each with six wings: with two wings they covered their faces, with two they covered their feet, and with two they were flying. And they were calling to one another:

"Holy, holy, holy is the LORD Almighty;
    the whole earth is full of his glory."

At the sound of their voices the doorposts and thresholds shook and the temple was filled with smoke.

"Woe to me!" I cried. "I am ruined! For I am a man of unclean lips, and I live among a people of unclean lips, and my eyes have seen the King, the LORD Almighty."

Then one of the seraphim flew to me with a live coal in his hand, which he had taken with tongs from the altar. With it he touched my mouth and said, "See, this has touched your lips; your guilt is taken away and your sin atoned for."

Then I heard the voice of the Lord saying, "Whom shall I send? And who will go for us?"

And I said, "Here am I. Send me!" (Isaiah 6:1–8)

Good stuff, yes?

On one level, it's a fantastic instance of the divine invading the realm of regular humans so that God can supernaturally call a prophet to His service.

But on another level, it's the story of every Christian. It is, if you will, an outline of the steps to maturity in the faith. It is certainly the sequence we must go through to hear, be prepared for, and join the calling of God for our lives.

Before you and I came to faith, we were carrying on with our lives, thinking we were fine. Then suddenly, we were confronted with a holy God. Whether through a slow dawning of awareness as we grew up in a Christian environment or through a crisis that led to a breakthrough of the heavenly clouds, most of us came to a moment when we realised with a start that God really is there and really takes notice of the likes of you and me.

When we encounter God in earnest, we're immediately struck by two things: His absolute holiness and our absolute unholiness by comparison. When we get a glimpse, as Isaiah did, of God's true nature, we're abashed, and we want to say, with Peter, "Go away from me, Lord; I am a sinful man!" (Luke 5:8b).

God tends to have that effect on people. When we see who He is, we instantly see who we're not.

But He doesn't reveal His holiness because He wishes to terrorise. No, when God confronts people with His holy character today, He holds reconciliation and redemption in His hands. It may pain (or even terrify) us to realise how far short of His standard we fall, but His aim is renewal. If we will receive the cleansing, He is pleased to give it.

Finally, with the enmity removed from between the person and God, He can move on to the real reason for the encounter. The Lord says to each of us, as He said to Isaiah, "I have a thing I need someone to do." Or, "Whom shall I send? And who will go for us?"

When we have been touched and cleansed by a holy God and we stand in deep gratitude for His redemption, our only answer can be, "Well, Lord, I'm standing right here—why not send me? Really, please send me. Surely You must send me!"

Which was, of course, the whole reason God made Himself known to the person in the first place.

God initiates, cleanses, calls, and commissions. That is the essence of the Christian experience.

Today, even now, God still has "a thing" He needs someone to do. He's calling you to be His hands and feet to bring that work to fruition. Will you answer His call?

A DIVINE ORDER

Here I Am is organised according to the shape of our passage from Isaiah 6.

Just as the opening verses of the passage depict Isaiah's sudden awareness that God was near and "up to something", chapter one examines your sense that God is calling you to something new.

As Isaiah was overwhelmed by the holiness of God's presence, so chapter two takes you into a healthy fear of the Lord as you are reminded of who God is.

As Isaiah cried out in his woe and awareness of his unclean lips, so chapter three guides you beyond the destructive power of sin in you, in others, and in society, and invites you to repentance.

In chapter four, mirroring when the Lord purified Isaiah from his sin by touching his lips with a coal, you will consider the good choices you can make to find yourself purified for service.

When Isaiah heard God say He had need of someone to go for Him, he was becoming aware of the work God needed done because of the ways in which men were breaking His heart. Chapter five is an intimate look at God's heart for the poor, marginalised, and lost.

Finally, chapter six brings you to the full ability to offer yourself to follow God's call into the work He has for you. It is your chance to say, "Here I am—send me!"

Throughout, you will read stories of men and women who have encountered God's holy presence, turned from their ways, and been sent out into the work of God through the ministry of The Message.

At the end of our journey together, I'm praying that your calling will be solidified and confirmed, the work will be clarified, and you will have all the courage you need to jump up and down, begging God to send you out to do His will.

USING *HERE I AM*

Here I Am is designed to be used individually and as a group.

We have created companion videos in which Andy Hawthorne unpacks the theme of each chapter, along with inspiring stories of people who have seen their lives transformed by the good news of the gospel. The videos can be used in your personal devotions or as an introduction if you're using this book as a group study.

The videos are available in an app called Here I Am, available in both the Apple and Google Play app stores for your iOS or Android device. In addition, all videos are available to stream from www.HereIAmMovement.com, where you will also find a link to the mobile apps.

When using this book in a group, we suggest encouraging people to read the chapter before arriving. In order to make leading a group through *Here I Am* an easy task, we suggest using the following structure:

> 1. Welcome and icebreaker. If your group all know each other well, this is the easy part. However, if you have new people or a new group, then spend a little time encouraging participants to introduce themselves. A welcoming refreshment and some quiet worship music played in the background can help to make people feel comfortable.

> 2. Play the video. Play the video from that week's chapter to the group, either streaming from the app or website to your set-top box or smart TV, or if that isn't possible playing through a laptop or something similar.

> 3. Discussion questions. Lead the group in a discussion using the "Group Discussion Questions"

provided at the end of each chapter as a guide. Encourage people to contribute, watching out for those who may want to share something but are nervous or shy, and not allowing the more confident participants to dominate the discussion.

4. Prayer and refreshments. Give time at the end for prayer if that is something your group is comfortable with. There may be those who have been moved or inspired to act on something following the discussion and are seeking support; there may be some who feel stirred to seek God and His will for them in their local neighbourhood. Finish with refreshments and a time of fellowship.

INTRODUCTION: GROUP DISCUSSION QUESTIONS

Here I Am is designed to be enjoyed alone or in a small discussion group setting. Each chapter includes questions to get thoughts and conversations started.

1. Discuss with your group what comes to mind when you read that you need to be a "See, I am doing a new thing" sort of person. What does this mean to you?

2. Does anything occur to you when you read that you need to be a "Do you not perceive it?" kind of believer? What does this mean to you?

3. What steps could you take to become more of a "Wild animals honour me" person? What does this mean to you?

4. What would make you a "Streams in the wasteland" or "Rivers in the desert" sort of Christian? What would make your church that sort of church?

5. If you add all four of those elements together, do you start getting a sense of what your own calling might entail?

6. As you read the passage from Isaiah 6, what stands out to you?

7. Describe an encounter you've had with God that comes closest to Isaiah's encounter with God in Isaiah 6.

Chapter 1

AWAKENED TO THE CALL

In the year that King Uzziah died, I saw the Lord, high and exalted,
seated on a throne; and the train of his robe filled the temple.

Isaiah 6:1

We don't know if this was a dream Isaiah had while lying in bed or a vision that came to him as he stood in the temple. But either way, I have to imagine that it came as a shock to Isaiah. There he was, having pleasant dreams or a nice day praying in the temple, and *boom*, God is there, throne and all, with a robe like a billowing cloud filling more and more of the space.

So it is with us. Before we came to Christ, we probably operated more or less blissfully with almost no communication with—or even awareness of—God. We went our separate ways. But then we became aware of Him somehow, and this eventually led to us believing in our hearts and confessing with our mouths that He is Lord (Romans 10:9). First, we were unaware of His proximity to us, and then we became very aware of it, as happened with Isaiah.

But this is also the sequence when we, as Christians already, begin to sense that God might be calling us to something else, to some higher or deeper work, in His service. We'd been going along happily, doing what we do, even serving the Lord to the best of our ability. And then something enters our thoughts or our awareness, and we start to see Him filling the temple again and coming near in a special way for a special reason.

It often occurs to us as a feeling of growing discontent. Not that we're tiring of walking on the narrow way. It's not greed or unhappiness but a sort of holy discontentment. The sense that God is up to something and it might possibly involve us, but when, oh when, will He reveal it to us? It's a feeling you can't shake that tells you something is wrong with the world that someone should do something about, and that maybe that someone should be you.

I suspect that may be why you're reading this book. I suspect you've got an itch you can't scratch. Some thought or need has come into your mind about what God might be calling you to—or you desire that He *would* call you to such a task. You sense (or hope) that God has some new work that is yours to do, but you can't quite reach it yet.

God *is* really calling you. There is a deeper work He's beckoning you into.

Not to put too fine a point on it, but the problem isn't that He's not calling but that we're not yet following.

DRIVEN TO DISTRACTION

Most of us are not actively looking for ways to avoid God's call. Quite the opposite! What holds us back more often is that we're just too busy doing other things. We are living distracted lives, and sometimes that whisper of holy discontent can be shouted down by the ordinary stuff of life, much like the thorns that choke the good seed in Jesus' parable (Matthew 13:1–8; Mark 4:1–9).

Modern, Western consumer culture, with its smartphones and on-demand programming, is perfectly calibrated to fill all our available space. It's a marvellous distraction that can and will drown out the "still small voice" of God.

The key drivers of our society are easy to see: self-centredness, consumerism, and celebrity obsession. If we're not careful, those characteristics can even leak into our worship when we gather as God's people.

Is there anything more blasphemous than walking out at the end of a Sunday morning service and saying, "I didn't get much out of the worship today"? But I bet you've said it—I have too. So easily we can forget that it's not about us. It's about Him.

How about consumerism in God's people? You can see it as people flit from church to church because one place doesn't give them what they want or what they think they need, or the leader says something that upsets them, or they don't like the music style, or they don't get on with this person or that pastor.

We shouldn't be miserable in the place we choose to worship, and we shouldn't stay with a church that is deviating from God's path. But neither should we adopt a please-me-or-else attitude that has us "shopping" for churches. Find one that is pretty good and plant yourself in it. Work from the inside to make it the church you'd like it to be. Build relationships and pursue God there. Commit.

And of course, we're far from immune from celebrity culture. Who's the hottest celebrity worship leader or preacher these days? What festival, event, or conference do we need to travel to just to see them? In so many ways, God's people end up mimicking what we see in the world.

You might be surprised to hear that these things are not new. This is what was going on in Isaiah's day too. Look at this from Isaiah chapter 1:

> "The multitude of your sacrifices—
> 　　what are they to me?" says the LORD.
> "I have more than enough of burnt offerings,
> 　　of rams and the fat of fattened animals;
> I have no pleasure
> 　　in the blood of bulls and lambs and goats …
> Stop bringing meaningless offerings!
> 　　Your incense is detestable to me.
> New Moons, Sabbaths and convocations—
> 　　I cannot bear your worthless assemblies …

Wash and make yourselves clean.
Take your evil deeds out of my sight;
stop doing wrong." (Isaiah 1:11, 13, 16)

Apparently, the people were really going for it. They were bringing a multitude of bulls, lambs, and goats for sacrifice. The language implies that they were giving way beyond what was required by the law. There was such a lavishness about their gatherings that we might think God would be pleased with them. And yet, the Lord tells them to stop! He calls their offerings *meaningless* (verse 13).

That must have confused the people. They were hosting extravagant festivals and feasts, new moon sabbaths, convocations … the lot. In our day, we might say they were spending their entire summer travelling from festival to festival, having a great time, thinking that they were praising the Lord. But He calls it all "a burden." He even says, "I hate these festivals" (see verse 14).

Why? Because while celebrating these festivals, they were harbouring sin. They themselves were still "doing wrong" and committing "evil deeds," so until they decided to "wash and make [themselves] clean," He wouldn't receive their offerings, and those sacrifices would remain detestable, worthless, and meaningless.

If you and I aren't hearing God's call to a deeper walk with Him or His invitation to important work, it might be because we've become similar to the people of Isaiah's day. It may be that we've let self-centredness, consumerism, and celebrity obsession distract us.

Well, if that's what's happened, then there is a remedy! It's never too late, while we still live, to get right with Jesus.

GETTING OUR EARS CHECKED

The very fact that you're reading this book gives me every confidence that, one, God *is* calling you to a deeper work, and two, there's a part of you that wants to do whatever He asks and whatever must be done to hear His call.

The Lord, throne and all, is filling the temple of your heart. You've had your awakening and you've sensed that God has come near. Here are some ideas for making sure you can see and hear Him fully.

First, deal with any known sin in your life. Sin will keep us separated from the voice of God and will cause our "sacrifices" to become meaningless while it stands between ourselves and the Lord. Sin causes us to be cut off from the power of the vine. So ask His forgiveness! Why wait? He is always pleased to give it to all who ask. Then we will see His robe filling the temple like a cloud.

Second, stay alert. The people of God should, as John Stott once said, have one eye on the Word and one eye on the world. We should come to the morning news headlines saying, "Lord, help me understand what's going on from Your perspective." If we do this, maybe God will build a greater expectancy in our hearts.

What a good thing it would be for the people of God if we thought, "Wow, Jesus may just return very soon." I think it would change everything. It would affect the fact that we play games with sin. It would affect the way we spend our money. Maybe it would even affect our evangelism—if we thought that we'd soon be with Jesus for all eternity and we had a part to play in getting other people there. It's a bit of a wake-up call for us, isn't it? So as you listen for the voice of God, do so with an eye on Christ's Second Coming, which—you never know—might happen a lot sooner than some people think (1 Thessalonians 5:2).

Third, identify what it is that made you start suspecting that God might be calling you to a new work or a new level of partnership with Him. Isaiah was going along fine as a preacher *before* he had this encounter with God. His first inkling that God was about to change his direction was the vision and his sudden awareness that God was coming near.

What was your awakening to this change? Was it, indeed, a holy discontent with your current situation? Was it a trauma or crisis in your life or in the life of someone you love? Was it a setback or disappointment that showed you that your expectations were not in line with reality? Was it a word from God Himself? Identify this, because it will become part of your story when you tell people what caused you to make the big change I suspect you could be about to make.

Fourth, take inventory of how the Lord has made and gifted you. There is a chance God might call you into an area in which you have virtually no natural or spiritual ability, if only to cause you to rely exclusively upon His enabling. But it's perhaps more likely that He will call you into work that makes use of your spiritual gifts, your personal passions, and your training and skills. He made you on purpose, after all.

So make some lists. We've included a blank Venn diagram in appendix 2. Use it to list, in the circles, your passions, your gifts, your training, your temperament, your skills, your experience, your connections, and the sorts of things God has used you to do in the past. Look for the overlapping of things you love to do and things you're gifted and/or trained to do.

It's not our job to winnow out the good works God has prepared beforehand for us to walk in (Ephesians 2:10). That's God's department. But it doesn't hurt to turn your mind to these characteristics of your life, because God often calls us to do further work in areas where He's already had us honing our skills. Maybe, with your eyes scanning about in this way, you'll more rapidly detect the manner in which He may be calling you.

WAKING UP TO YOUR DESTINY

Sometimes it takes another person to wake us up to our destiny. Sometimes an entire group can sense God's calling on our lives, even if we don't, and they can invite us to see for ourselves what is clear to them.

That's what happened to Natasha Pollitt, a young woman in the neighbourhood of Hattersley in inner-city Manchester.

The Message has developed groups of believers who move into low-income districts—called "estates"—with the purpose of reaching at-risk young people, many of whom are already deep into addictions and crime, for the gospel. We call these groups *Eden teams*. It was the "Eden Hattersley" team that encountered young Natasha and was used by God to bring about her awakening. Here is Natasha's story in her own words:

Natasha Pollitt's Story

Before the Eden team came to Hattersley, my family life was quite chaotic. There was quite a lot of physical and emotional abuse growing up. As I became a teenager, at the most crucial point of trying to figure life out, I still felt a lot of fear and anger. I wasn't the most well-behaved, due to the environment I was in. So at the age of 14, when the Eden team arrived, I was at a point where I was suffering depression. My parents had just split up, as well. I didn't know what I wanted to do, and I had no plans for the future. I just thought I'd be on benefits for the rest of my life. As a coping mechanism, I was drinking and taking drugs to try and get rid of what I was feeling. I just didn't feel confident without taking something.

I remember meeting the Eden team for the first time and feeling quite excited. I could see something in them that was different and very appealing. On the other hand, I was in a different world. My friends thought they were brainwashing me with the faith side of stuff. It wasn't until later on that I was able to grasp the Christian faith. Before then, I'd had no great experience of faith. Sometimes I'd gone to church just because we'd get a Sunday dinner afterwards. But I'd never really thought about it.

Initially, I tested them with my behaviour because I found it difficult to trust anyone. I wasn't disruptive, but I was quite cheeky. I desperately wanted to hear more about their Christian faith, but I didn't trust what they had to say. My mum also said she didn't want me to be any part of them. But when I was with them, I felt different and wanted to know more. They seemed to see something in me, some worth or purpose, that I didn't see in myself. So I kept going to their youth meetings.

Over the next five years, they became a major part of my world. They didn't just invite me to church and chat to me, either—they stepped in at a time when I needed major medical surgery. It wasn't my parents taking me to these appointments; it was the Eden team. They became family. They became people I wanted to be like.

When I was 19, the Eden team leader, Sharon Murphy, said I should get out of the area where I lived so I could be free from my friends, who were still taking drugs. It was the lifestyle that I couldn't get out of. So I moved to Old Trafford to be part of Message Academy (at that time, called Genetik) run by The Message Trust. But even then, I was scared to trust God. The turning point came when I went on a six-month mission trip to Zimbabwe with The Message.

When I told my mum I wanted to go to Africa for half a year, she said if I went there I couldn't come home. But for the first time, I felt like God was calling me to do something. Being away in a different country is where I found my faith. When I was there helping others, I was free to be who I was. No one was taking drugs or drinking alcohol. I left the airport a smoker, but over there we weren't able to smoke. So a lot of my lifestyle changed, and that's when I grasped God fully. I awakened to the reality that there was a God, and I could see Him in other people's lives.

When I came back from Africa, I moved back into Hattersley Estate and, unfortunately, the same cycle began as the same temptations came back. Then Sharon told me they were creating an Eden team in Sheffield, and she asked me if I'd become one of their youth workers. I took the opportunity to get out of Manchester.

But I soon discovered I couldn't run away from all the hurt and pain. One evening, I was sexually assaulted by two men. I remember walking the streets afterwards just crying. I had never felt so alone. I didn't know what to do or who would help me.

Then I remembered that the Eden team was always there, so I called Sharon. She came with her husband and brought me back to her house. I never spoke to her about what happened. I didn't tell anyone, because I believed at that time that it was my fault. When I was with her, I knew I was safe. She arranged for the team to be with me the next day.

There were similar situations that my lifestyle led me into, as I continued on a cycle of drinking, drugs, suicide idolisation, and self-harm. I believed those "solutions" were helping me to cope with the emotional pain I had been carrying from childhood. But I finally realised they were harming me even more.

That was what made me decide to go into the City Hearts Restore programme in Sheffield, which helps vulnerable women deal with abuse and addictions. During my time with City Hearts Restore, I was able to talk about how it had been at home and what I'd been through, and I had the freedom to let everything out. After completing the programme, I found I was finally free from my past.

Over the years since then, I've been trained in counselling and dealing with people with addictive behaviours, and now I'm working there full-time. I'm an assistant coordinator for the City Hearts Restore programme, working with women with life-controlling issues such as self-harm, eating disorders, depression, and drug and alcohol abuse. Also, I'm a case worker for the anti-trafficking side of City Hearts Restore.

It's indescribable when I look back to how I was when I was in a place of wanting to end my life and having low self-worth. I can honestly say that all of that is now completely gone. When I sit with women, I just see it as such an honour and privilege to be in the place that I am at.

I'm so grateful that the Eden team came into my life. If they hadn't come to my estate, I'd still be where I was with no hope for a future. But they saw something in me and called it out in me. Now I am helping other women step out of fear and into the freedom I've found.

HERE I AM. SEND ME!

What was it that made you pick up this book? Was it that you have always loved this passage in Isaiah? (I love it too!) Was it that you sense God calling you to a bigger life—or you'd like to *have* Him call you to a bigger life? Was it that you've heard of me or The Message or The World Wide Message Tribe or our work in the UK or elsewhere? Did someone give it to you as a gift? In any case, I'm glad you're here.

Now let me ask a better question: What has God called you to do? God invites every one of His children into His work. Did you know that? You don't have to be a seminary-trained Bible scholar to be the very hands of Jesus on this earth.

There are many ways to answer the question of what God has called you to do. You can say that He's called you to love and serve Him, and that's absolutely true. You can say that He's called you to use your spiritual gifts in the local church, and that's true. You can say you must bloom where you're planted and shine your light wherever you are, which is surely so. You can say you must simply look around yourself and see what needs doing, or what Jesus would do, or where God is already working, and then do what your conscience compels you to do, and that would be brilliant.

But many people long for a larger work, a calling that will demand everything of them and be much, much too big for them, that only God's enabling will allow them to do.

Is that you? Do you long to hear God saying, "Whom shall I send? And who will go for us?" Are you electrified by the very prospect of volunteering—sight unseen—for whatever God might call you to do?

How rarely do most of us enter into such a posture of willingness to be sent *wherever* to do *whatever*! And when we are in that posture, how we yearn for God to instantly hand over to us our orders, our itinerary, and our plane tickets.

In an upcoming chapter, you're going to read the story of a woman who says that you must "be quietly, stubbornly determined to use all your skills to bring justice, mercy, and kingdom" to the world. That's what we want, isn't it? We want to be all-in on a job that is epic and massive, holding on with all our strength to God's own hand as He leads us into the hurts and darkness of a lost world.

Isaiah had a dramatic awakening to the nearness of God. It's as if the veil grew thin and God's form could be seen pressing against it and His voice could be heard. It was a moment when the holiest of holies in the temple suddenly enveloped Isaiah, and he was in God's own fiery presence.

What is your level of awareness of God's nearness right now? Do you sense His closeness more than usual? Less than usual? About the same? Stop your activity, stop your thoughts, and dwell before the Lord. Ask Him to come near. Ask for eyes to see and ears to hear and a heart wide open to His will. Plead for your own awakening.

And just wait. Simply dwell in that stillness. Discipline your thoughts to be silent. Ignore the distractions. Sit. Wait. Abide.

Listen.

CHAPTER 1: GROUP DISCUSSION QUESTIONS

1. What caused you to pick up this book? What caused your group to choose to go through it?

2. Is there an "itch you can't scratch," a holy discontentment, that is causing you to wonder if God might be calling you to something bigger than what you're currently doing? Answer for yourself but also in terms of something your group might do together.

3. In what ways can you see self-centredness, consumerism, and/or celebrity obsession in the church? In what ways can you see those things in your own life?

4. What things have you seen in the news or the world around you that you think might indicate that we are closer (or perhaps *no* closer) to the Second Coming of Christ? What's the consensus in the group?

5. If you did a Venn diagram or inventory of your own life, gifts, skills, passions, education, and experience, what sort of thing would you venture to guess that God's calling on your life might involve? (Note that we have included a Venn diagram template in appendix 2.)

Chapter 2

OVERWHELMED BY THE HOLY

Above him were seraphim, each with six wings: with two wings
they covered their faces, with two they covered their feet, and
with two they were flying. And they were calling to one another:
"Holy, holy, holy is the LORD Almighty; the whole earth is full
of his glory." At the sound of their voices the doorposts and
thresholds shook and the temple was filled with smoke.

Isaiah 6:2–4

As Isaiah sat praying in the temple, the Lord arrived in all His glory,
surrounded by worshipping angelic beings. This was almost certainly
a manifestation of Jesus Himself as we shall one day see Him (see

John 12:41). Hundreds of years before He was born in Bethlehem, Jesus was already on His throne ruling the world.

The first stage in an encounter with God is the dawning awareness that He has drawn near in an unusual way. That's the awakening to His presence that we talked about in chapter one.

The second stage is a fresh confrontation with the true character of God. Isaiah had an encounter with His fiery holiness. Later in this same episode, Isaiah will glimpse the compassionate love of the Lord—but first comes holiness.

So it is with us. We must be reminded of the purity of God, His goodness and "otherness," or we will forget that He is God. I think it's fair to say that modern preaching can sometimes go too far in making Jesus relatable, turning Him into a toothless wimp who is so eager to forgive that He just winks at sin and gives out goodies. A fresh encounter with God's holiness will renew our understanding that there are global, universal, *eternal* matters at stake and that the One at the reins of them all is higher and beyond us. That He is a being of epic proportions, a God worthy of our obedience and service.

SOME OR ALL?

When this holy God looks out over all of humanity, what does He see?

He sees those who are currently His and those who are not currently His. He sees those who are moving toward Him and those who are running away from Him. He sees sins and He sees the blood of

Jesus over all. Sinners, saints, backsliders, the demonically oppressed, and the pure of heart. He sees the full range of possible positions on the continuum of man's relation to God. And He sees them with a spectrum of colours and an array of lenses that you and I can never have, at least this side of eternity.

Indeed, when you and I look out over humanity, we often don't have God's eyesight at all. We don't know who is His and who is not, despite what conclusions we may draw or what the people themselves may protest. We don't know our own hearts, let alone anyone else's. And if there really is a group who are heaven bound and a group who are not, we don't know that either.

By preventing us from discerning who is "in" and who is "out," God has forced us to do what we should be doing anyway, which is to assume that every single person we meet has a real, legitimate chance of coming to Christ and entering into eternity with Him.

As far as we're concerned, God has chosen everybody. We must look out across humanity and assume that God wants everybody to be saved. Paul tells us as much:

> God our Saviour ... wants all people to be saved and to come to a knowledge of the truth. (1 Timothy 2:3b–4)

> The Lord's servant must not be quarrelsome but must be kind to everyone, able to teach, not resentful. Opponents must be gently instructed, in the

hope that God will grant them repentance leading
them to a knowledge of the truth, and that they will
come to their senses and escape from the trap of the
devil, who has taken them captive to do his will.
(2 Timothy 2:24–26)

We're not going to get worked up about whether they're chosen
or not, since we can't know. We're just going to love everybody. We're
just going to give all people a drink from the river of life-giving water.

ARE WE NICER THAN GOD?

Journeying through the first few chapters of Isaiah really got me
thinking: Are we sometimes, as Gerald Coates has put it, "nicer than
God"? Of course, our God is all-loving and full of mercy. But He is
also a holy and fearful judge who must therefore punish sin.

When I committed my life to Christ over forty years ago, I
was given a classic tract called "Journey into Life" (written in 1964
by Norman Warren, and still published today). Inside, there was a
picture of a coin that sought to represent the two sides of God's
character. One side of the coin had the word "Love" imprinted on it,
and the other side said "Justice."

It's crucial that we understand that God is both, and that we hold
both God's love and God's justice in balance in our own theology. If
we teach only the "love" side of the coin, we end up with a distorted,
weak gospel. Why? Because without God being holy, perfect, and
demanding of justice, He would have no right to call us to abstain

from sin. He would have no right to call us to obedience. Further, if God weren't a holy judge who condemned sin, Jesus would not have had to die. Indeed, His death would've been worthless and meaningless. Jesus died on the cross to face the full judgement and wrath that we deserved, in the face of a holy, perfect God.

God is also fully loving, and of course love will have the last word. If we teach only God's justice and holiness, we depict Him as an angry, spiteful God who will delight to send people into eternal flames of damnation. That's clearly not our God.

Balance is what we need. And we need to remember that the so-called "gentle Jesus, meek and mild," spoke more about hell than He did about heaven. Why? Because He didn't want anyone to go there! His life was one great rescue mission, both from hellish lives now and from the penalty of hell in the future.

That same Jesus who classically said in John 3:16, "For God so loved the world that he gave his one and only Son, that whoever believes in him shall not perish but have eternal life," also said a few verses later in John 3:36, "Whoever believes in the Son has eternal life, but whoever rejects the Son will not see life, for God's wrath remains on them." We like one of those quotes a lot more than the other, don't we? But both are equally true.

It was this sense of saving people from God's righteous wrath and judgement that has historically sent so many missionaries to travel all over the world. But it was with a heart of love and the gospel message of good news that they went out too. Our job is not to be gloomy, sour-faced miseries telling people what sinners they are, but to be a people blown away by what we've been saved from and committing ourselves with total abandon to playing our part in God's great rescue mission.

When God filled the temple and bowled Isaiah over with His presence, it was His holiness that got his attention. The love of God is the compassion that motivates us to soften our hearts toward those in need of mercy (and that's everyone!). But it is the justice of God that compels us to act. To use a metaphor, it's as if we see a child who has wandered onto a thoroughfare. We want to act to save the child. Likewise, our desires that all people 1) find mercy and 2) escape punishment are intermixed as we look out across humanity, and in this mixture we hope to have something close to the perspective of God.

JESUS PREACHED REPENTANCE

In our Christian culture today, God's justice has fallen out of favour. It's considered impolite to speak about holiness or repentance. Spiritual disciplines are often seen as too difficult—or as curiosities pursued by only the most zealous. The way to seem relevant is to talk of the *love* and "tolerance" of Christ, depicting Him as nonviolent and as close to Gandhi-likeness as possible. Millennials won't listen, we're told, to a message of stringent holiness or justice, and we're encouraged to hurry back to words of God's all-accepting nature. Because who would follow an intolerant God? Honestly, in this day and age.

Christians, in this way no different from non-Christians, seem to need constant reassurances about their worth. The most popular worship songs seem to be about the unending love of God. It's as if God's love leaks out of us, so we have to keep surrounding ourselves with frequent reminders and assurances that He loves us. Now, God certainly does love us with an unending love, and I'm not sure I want a flurry of new songs depicting the fires of hell. But this state of affairs is extremely out of balance, and it shows how the church has embraced (perhaps unconsciously) the cultural demand that God be accepting and, above all else, non-judgemental.

Yet Jesus preached repentance all the time. Everywhere Jesus went, He left penitents in His wake. It was not only John the Baptist who preached repentance, after all. Here are our Lord's own words as He summed up His ministry: "The kingdom of God has come near. Repent and believe the good news!" (Mark 1:15b).

Jesus preached repentance because He hated sin with every fibre of His being. Why did He weep when he looked on Jerusalem (Luke 19:41)? Because He saw the destructive effects of sin on His people, and He just longed to gather them up so they could be forgiven and free. And He did everything that was necessary for that to happen. His impulse was love, certainly, but it was to *save from judgement* that He acted.

Look at the beauty of people who pursue righteousness and holiness and don't allow sin to tangle them. Yes, they sin, but they quickly repent. They walk in repentance. They get time with the Lord every day to allow the illuminating Holy Spirit to reveal to them what's wrong and what offends Him, because they hate sin. They do it because they want to be at the cutting edge of God's purposes. They don't want to miss out or be set aside or passed over for any of His tasks. They want to know the fullness of the Holy Spirit, and they understand that the Holy Spirit fully fills only holy people.

That's what The Message is about. We're not primarily about running a charity; we're about rescuing people from hell. We're about removing the destructive, deadly force of sin in this generation, and the only way it can be removed is through the blood of Jesus.

The word "holy" in the Bible simply means to be set apart for special use. When your mum serves dinner on the everyday plates, you think nothing of it. But when she pulls out the fine china, you know a special time has come.

When God calls someone to special service, He begins by sanctifying—by "making holy"—the servant. When the Spirit called Barnabas and Paul to their first missionary journey, He said, "**Set apart** for me Barnabas and Saul for the work to which I have called them" (Acts 13:2b, emphasis mine). They were to be set in a special spot, made holy, set apart specially for a mighty work.

Jesus sanctified (made holy) His disciples simply by teaching in their presence. As they placed themselves under the flow of those holy-making words, as they remained within the effect of the teachings and took them to heart, it purified them, syllable by syllable (John 15:3). Those who would not tolerate the holy words had to run away or silence them (Acts 7:54–58).

> For the word of God is alive and active. Sharper
> than any double-edged sword, it penetrates even
> to dividing soul and spirit, joints and marrow; it

judges the thoughts and attitudes of the heart.
(Hebrews 4:12)

You and I don't need to put on sackcloth and ashes and stand
in the city square with a "TURN OR BURN!" sign. But neither
can we shy away from holiness, whether it be the holiness of God
Himself or the holy-making work He desires to do in us. If we
would say, "Here I am! Send me!" we must first be set apart for His
holy use.

So what about you? What is your stance on God's holiness in
the world? In the church? On your smartphone? What things do
you do and not do as a result of your awareness of the pure fire of
Christ? Not that an external focus on the "Do not handle ... Do
not touch" (Colossians 2:21) rules has any value at all. But God's
righteousness ought to show up in His children, don't you think?

TURNING ONE HUNDRED EIGHTY DEGREES

A changed life has a power we can never estimate or predict.
There's a reason Jesus often sent those He healed back to their
villages and families. It's one thing for a stranger to claim healing or change; it's something else entirely for someone you've
known for years to show up living differently and displaying true
righteousness.

Nick and Andrea Shahlavi are a great example of this. Both
had been living hard and dissolute lives. But then Nick got radi-
cally saved, and Andrea began to take notice. Here's their story in
Andrea's words:

Nick and Andrea Shahlavi's Story

My brother and I were brought up by our mum on an estate in Collyhurst Village, Manchester. It was a rough area, but my mum did her best. My dad was hardly ever around when I was growing up. From the age of 11 I got into drink. We used to go to the shops

during school breaks and buy alcohol, and then the drinking continued out of school.

In time, I got into drugs and became addicted to speed and cocaine. I left home when I was just 17. To pay my rent and feed my addiction, I was doing anything to make some money, including dealing drugs, selling stolen goods, and looking after guns for people. I also worked in hospitals doing the laundry on night shifts. But as my addiction continued, I got into a lot of debt and was constantly dodging drug dealers I owed money to. It got so bad that I actually spent my 18th birthday in a police cell for beating my mum up because she wouldn't give me money for drugs.

I tried to overcome my addiction by moving away to Blackpool, where I worked in a hotel. But I was feeling very low and had no friends to turn to at all.

On two occasions, I even tried to end my life by jumping off the pier. But each time, someone stopped me. I now believe that this was God intervening in my life.

My dad was only barely in my life. He would come and visit me from time to time throughout my childhood, just to give me a present or money. When I was so low in Blackpool, I remember calling him. For the first time, he told me he loved me and I started breaking down.

After about a year, I moved back to Manchester and worked at a gambling arcade where I would give people change for the slot machines. That was where I met my future husband, Nick. He was also on drugs at the time, and he was a drug dealer and a gambler. I was living in a basement and Nick had nowhere to stay, so he came to stay with me ... and he never left.

At the time, I was still on drugs and Nick was dealing drugs and smoking weed. We used to fight a lot, and one time he came home beaten up because drug dealers had taken his drugs off him. I was still on cocaine when I found out I was pregnant with my daughter, Alexis. I never took it again.

Then suddenly a miracle happened: Nick became a Christian and just wouldn't stop talking to me about God and the Bible. For me, having a drug dealer boyfriend who suddenly started talking about God all the time ... well, I thought he'd lost the plot.

What really changed him was when he started working at The Message Trust. He'd known Andy Hawthorne from years before, and he'd gone to see him, saying that he'd do anything, including clean the toilets, just to get into evangelism ministry. What was crazy was that I remembered The World Wide Message Tribe coming to my school when I was about 11. I didn't put my hand up then, but that was probably when a seed was first sown in me. What we didn't realise till later was that, while Andy was coming to my school, he was doing the same with Nick's.

What really turned me around was when I met Jane Sullivan at The Message in 2011. Nick introduced me to her in the prayer room one day. After chatting for a while, she asked me if I knew who Jesus was. I said no, I didn't. She told me in a nice calm way about God's love for me. At one point, she said He could be like my father, and I froze. Who would want that? She told me that *this* Father would never let me down. So I gave my life to the Lord in that prayer room.

Then she told me about the charity she was working for: CRMI Children of Hope. She asked me if I wanted to go to Uganda, which is where I'd always wanted to go to help children. That June, we flew out to Uganda on my first mission trip.

Just a few months later, Nick and I got married.

My faith changed how I looked at Nick. Now I saw him wanting to be a good father, because I didn't have that growing up. I saw him wanting the best for us. Also, my relationship with my mum changed for the better.

My dad passed away a few years ago, but a year after the wedding I was able to introduce him to my daughter, Alexis. He apologised for being absent all those years. I was able to forgive him for keeping his other family life away from me and for keeping me a secret from them all those years. Forgiveness really does set the forgiver free.

Since that first mission trip to Uganda, I've not stopped going. I go twice a year. What's amazing is now I've taken over much of the work of Children of Hope. I just can't imagine my life without the charity being in it. I treat the children like they're my own. They call me even "Mama Andrea".

My life used to be all about me, but now I just want to help others and give back.

I'm so thankful that Andy Hawthorne and The Message believed in Nick. Now he's part of the hip-hop missions team Vital Signs at The Message. I believe this is where I am supposed to be. I'm so thankful that God not only saved my life but He's given me an opportunity to save other lives.

HERE I AM. SEND ME!

"The fear of the LORD is the beginning of wisdom, and knowledge of the Holy One is understanding" (Proverbs 9:10).

We don't talk much these days about the fear of the Lord. In our modern culture, we like our lords inclusive, tolerant, and fluffy, thank you very much. Were a contemporary Jonathan Edwards to preach "Sinners in the Hands of an Angry God," he'd be called a bigot and shown the door.

That's not to say that many Christians haven't abused the fear of the Lord and turned it into legalism, control, and, quite frankly, hatred. Indeed, many have. For good reason has the idea of a vengeful God who doesn't mind tossing sinners into the eternal fire become unpopular. But neither would a defanged, de-holied God be worth serving.

The solution isn't to throw out either but to find the place of balance for both.

Isaiah had a full-on encounter with the living God. Mysterious creatures. Heavenly voices. A temple full of smoke. Shaking doorposts beneath the footsteps of the Almighty.

When was the last time you had a visitation like that? But all of us can pursue the throne and plead with God to unveil His holiness, at least in part.

How lax we become when we lose sight of His holiness! How we wink at sin when we forget His fiery purity! How like chaff we would be consumed if we were exposed to it fully, and yet how easily we set it aside.

You have volunteered to follow the leading of your Lord. As you prepare to hear the actual content of His call, as you ready your heart and sharpen the ears of your spirit, seek His holiness! Ask Him to cleanse and purify you, even from forgotten sin, and to enliven your soul again with the fear of the Lord.

CHAPTER 2: GROUP DISCUSSION QUESTIONS

1. Why do you agree or disagree that God's judgement and holiness are as important to remember and teach as His love? What if that causes those around you to claim you are being intolerant?

2. "Christians shouldn't need to be constantly reassured of Christ's love for them." Does the group agree with that statement? Why or why not? What causes the "need" in the first place? Does God's love leak out of us? Do we secretly believe that God is wrong to love us? What might enable Christians to move on from being stuck in the spot of continually asking, "Does God really love me?" to the freedom of saying, "Because God's love for me is settled forever, how can I go out and serve Him in the power of His love"?

3. How does the group react to this statement: "If I knowingly allow sin to remain in my life, God will pass over me and give someone else the task—or even the calling—He had originally wanted to give to me"?

4. When the Apostle Paul, who had been willing to travel far and wide to persecute those who followed Christ, became a Christian and was set apart by the Spirit to travel far and wide to *lead* people to Christ, I speculate that he felt he'd finally discovered what he'd been created to do. In *Chariots of Fire,* Eric Liddell said that God had made him fast for a purpose, "And when I run, I feel His pleasure." When we come into our calling, we have this sense that we have found what God had crafted us to do and be when He made us. Discuss with the group what might be, as you look over your life and your giftings and passions, God's calling for you.

Chapter 3

AWARE OF OUR OWN SIN

*"Woe to me!" I cried. "I am ruined! For I am a man of
unclean lips, and I live among a people of unclean lips,
and my eyes have seen the King, the LORD Almighty."*

Isaiah 6:5

Our only possible reaction to an encounter with the holiness of
God is a heart-piercing realisation of our own sinfulness. I don't
care if it's Mother Teresa, St. Francis of Assisi, John Wesley, or the
Apostle Paul, no human can match the holiness of the great I Am.
Even if we're not usually given to comparison, seeing ourselves so

far below the glory of God is as inevitable as it is sobering. But I think it's healthy to be reminded of who God is ... and who we aren't.

Isaiah got a glimpse of the hidden world of heaven, a world that is just as real as the one we can see. Though we are almost never aware of the fact, all around us are angels and archangels, principalities and powers, and maybe even the odd seraph—which literally means "burning one."

These heavenly beings are our role models for worship. They never lose sight of who is God and who is not. Take a look at the angelic beings in Isaiah 6: They were not just calling to the Lord, which we might think would be enough to honour Him. Rather, they were also encouraging one another as they sang: "Holy, Holy, Holy is the Lord Almighty, the whole earth is filled with his glory." This is a lesson for us. When we get together, there needs to be a horizontal aspect to our worship as well as a vertical one. We are to spur one another on by our passion and desire for the Lord.

We are also to look for the glory of the Lord everywhere, because the whole earth—not just our meeting house—is filled with His train. But meeting the holy is not for the faint of heart.

UNCLEAN LIPS

Have you ever come face to face with your own inadequacy? Perhaps you're asked to do a task that is clearly beyond your ability. Maybe you're presented with a bill you cannot possibly pay.

Many fathers report feeling a rising panic as they hold their first baby in their arms and the awareness settles upon them that they are now the chief agent of protection and provision for a living human being.

Such moments have a sobering, and sometimes unpleasant, effect on us. They represent a wake-up call as arresting as cold water thrown in our face. And yet, this is the way of preparation to serve the Most High.

As all this worship went on in the temple, things got more than a little scary for Isaiah. The doorposts shook! The temple filled with smoke! He genuinely thought he was a dead man.

I'm reminded of Job when he had a similar encounter with the I Am:

> The LORD said to Job:
>
> "Will the one who contends with the Almighty
> > correct him?
> Let him who accuses God answer him!"
>
> Then Job answered the LORD:
>
> "I am unworthy—how can I reply to you?
> I put my hand over my mouth.
> I spoke once, but I have no answer—
> > twice, but I will say no more. ..."

My ears had heard of you
>   but now my eyes have seen you.
Therefore I despise myself
>   and repent in dust and ashes."
>   (Job 40:1–5; 42:5–6)

When Isaiah was confronted with the consuming holiness of God, all he could think of saying was, "Woe to me! I am ruined! For I am a man of unclean lips, and I live among a people of unclean lips." In that place of utter glory, he became keenly aware of his lack of purity and holiness.

For the first five chapters of his book, Isaiah had pretty much been breathing fire and speaking woe to the Jewish people. Here's a taste:

Jerusalem staggers,
>   Judah is falling;
their words and deeds are against the LORD,
>   defying his glorious presence.
The look on their faces testifies against them;
>   they parade their sin like Sodom;
>   they do not hide it.
Woe to them!
>   They have brought disaster upon themselves.
>   (Isaiah 3:8–9)

But suddenly, in the presence of the majestic awesomeness of the Lord, the spotlight turns upon Isaiah. And all he can find to say is, "I am unclean!" Not "Woe to them" anymore, but "Woe to *me!*"

Isaiah realises that it's not just Israel that is sinful. And yet, isn't that how many Christians behave sometimes—as if everyone else is the problem? I know I've been guilty of that. But when we see ourselves in light of the Lord's holiness, we see that we, too, are black with sin and in desperate need of a Saviour.

This is the place we need to pray that people will get to. Because, without a genuine sense of our own sin-sickness, how can anyone truly turn to the only One who can heal them?

One of the reasons I love our prison work so much is that you don't usually need to convince inmates that they are sinners or that they need a Saviour. They already know. And it's often as easy as shelling peas to get them to the place of real repentance.

Sinfulness is the human condition. In Christ, we are cleansed and forgiven, it is true. But we must never believe that our redeemed state is something we ourselves accomplished or can be proud of. Christians were once as non-Christians are now, and there is no virtue or merit we can hold over those who have not yet received it. As Paul wrote:

> For who makes you different from anyone else? What do you have that you did not receive? And if you did receive it, why do you boast as though you did not? (1 Corinthians 4:7)

It is a sobering truth that one day everyone we will ever meet will be in the same position Isaiah found himself in: confronted by a holy God. But Isaiah had a chance to repent. I'm afraid that, when this day comes for so many, it will be too late to receive forgiveness.

Surely that's got to spur us on to get out there and tell some people the life-changing good news! Surely that will send us running out to tell everyone that the "holy, holy, holy" One got down from His throne, came to earth, showed us what God is like, died on a cross to be punished for all the sins of all time, then rose again and conquered death once and for all.

I think I feel a "Hallelujah!" coming on!

Judgement and mercy have to be held in balance, as I've said. God's holiness and God's love must be delicately interwoven. Stress His compassion too much, and people wink at sin and go on hurting themselves and others. Stress His righteousness too much, and people can think they will never be accepted into heaven.

So many Christians are crippled by guilt. Why should this be? Many times, it is because our friends the angels and archangels aren't the only spiritual beings watching us. The devil and his nasty minions are at work too. Their plan is to accuse us, condemn us, lie to us, and keep us in defeat, trapped by our past. We need to remember at all times that Jesus has forgiven us, chosen not to remember our sins, and has a bright and triumphant future for us.

When you have your awakening—either to come to faith in Christ in the first place or in a later encounter when God draws near as He did with Isaiah—and when you have all your calibrations reset so that you see yourself in light of the towering holiness and forgiveness of God Almighty, there really is only one response. To fall down and worship.

As Isaiah was worshipping, there was love in his attitude, certainly, but also a great "fear of the Lord." His was the response of the man who finds all his shameful deeds suddenly thrown open before a judge. His worship carried more than a hint of mortification. But I can't escape the conclusion that this is the correct reaction to a true meeting with God.

And I can't help noticing that my own worship is hardly ever like this.

WHERE IS OUR HOLINESS?

I say to the team at The Message that the most important thing they bring to the work is their holiness. We might have great facilities, great creativity, great sacrifices, even great sacrificial prayer going on and yet still miss out on God's maximum if it's not all built on the platform of holy lives before God.

Perhaps now, more than at any other time in my Christian life, everywhere I look I see people not taking sin seriously—and we are all suffering the consequences. Even small sins can hold us back in massive ways.

We can't play games with sin. It will devour us. Electricity is a great gift that makes all kinds of fun things possible: movie theatres, amusement park rides, smartphones, and the rest. But relate to electricity wrongly, and it will hurt you. It could very easily kill you.

If I saw a child bending down to pick up a downed power cable, I wouldn't stand by and watch him die. I wouldn't encourage him. I wouldn't tell him, with a shrug, that it might not be the best idea for him. No! I'd rugby tackle him.

We need to be in accountability with each other, and if we see a brother or sister playing with sin, we need to step in boldly.

"Your kingdom come, your will be done, on earth as it is in heaven" (Matthew 6:10) is first of all a personal prayer, after all. When we're praying for God's rule and reign to come on the earth, shouldn't they happen in our own hearts first? We must be manifesting holy lives.

Lord, confront us again with Your merciful, terrible, redeeming holiness!

JUDGEMENT LEADS TO REPENTANCE

The purpose of God's judgement is always restoration. The theme of the whole book of Isaiah is that God will have a people and His purposes will prevail. Not, "God will have a people and then destroy them." When He brings judgement, it's in support of that goal. He may have to judge His own people, but never to cut them off entirely. He will always leave at least a remnant (Isaiah 11). His heart is always to bring them to repentance. And if He judges the surrounding nations, it's always at least partially to warn His own people to remain holy before Him.

Throughout the book of Isaiah, you'll see the theme of judgement time and time again. There are prophecies against Moab to the east, against Philistia to the west, against Egypt to the south, and against Syria to the north. Each prophecy carries the same tension—of judgement leading to salvation. Fire and fearful judgement come, yes, but it's all part of God working out His purposes, ultimately leading to His salvation plan.

Repentance that leads to blessing ... this is what the Lord is looking for, both then and now. God does not delight in the destruction of anyone. His goal is always new or restored fellowship and the strengthening of His people.

Through Isaiah, God was warning His children: "Whatever you do, do not live like those around you. Do not live like those to the north, east, south, and west, who are worshipping things made by their own hands, who are given over to sin, who are going down a road of destruction. Live differently. Repent!"

It's the same today, 3,000 years later. We need to learn that our personal repentance is central to our wider purpose. No holiness in the heart, no positive impact in the world.

If we want to live inside the big vision God has for us—and make no mistake, God is calling you and me to something big—then we must walk in repentance. If we want to see the gospel proclaimed, communities transformed, prisoners set free, and lives redeemed, we need to hate sin. We need to look at the cultures and communities and nations around us and say, "We're not going to live like that. We're going to stand out as different."

Satan is subtle and seductive, and he's always got another step down for us. He's always got an even more nasty, more dirty image on the computer screen. He's always got another door we can open into addiction. He's always got another way to trigger us or another excuse for us to play victim and act out of entitlement. His goal has ever been to steal, kill, and destroy. To hinder God's plan. To discourage and derail God's servants. He has not taken a vacation and he has not changed.

If we want to be a useful part of God's big plan, we've got to be a people who say, "No, I'm going to be quick to repent of that stuff. I'm not going to go there. Why would I want to go there when I've got a bigger, wider purpose? I've joined God's adventurous call to love the world. Back off, Satan, in the name of Jesus! I've chosen to make a mark in this generation. I choose holiness."

TRUE REPENTANCE

Christians tend to go to one of two extremes when they talk about sin. Either they turn to legalism: "Don't smoke, don't drink, don't dance, don't go to the sin-ema!" Or (much more likely in this generation) they turn to license and become lax about sex, drink, or whatever it is.

The Bible talks about sin a lot, but we don't talk about it enough.

I first got serious about God when I was seventeen. Before that, I'd become a rebel at school. In fact, I was told by the headmaster that I was the worst pupil that had ever been to the school. I was quite proud of that, really.

Then I met the Lord, and everything changed. I mean, everything. When the RE (Religious Education) teacher at the school heard that Andy Hawthorne, the worst pupil, the nightmare kid, had become a Christian—and not just a Christian but a raving evangelist who was going "round to all the pubs in Cheadle witnessing and trying to lead his mates to Jesus left, right, and centre"—he phoned me up. "Would you come in and take a day of RE lessons?"

At this point, I'd been a full-on Christian for only a few weeks, so I was a bit taken aback by his call. But I said okay, and the next thing I knew, I was standing in my school for back-to-back lessons giving my testimony for an hour at a time.

I thought to make it a little more engaging, so I brought along a boom box with a cassette of an Irish Christian punk band (Andy McCarroll & Moral Support's album *Zionic Bonds*) and played a song called 'Sin.' It talks about how cancerous sin is and how it will kill you. It was great. After three minutes of loud punk, I said, "Actually, I believe that. I believe sin kills. It's cancer. It will destroy you. It separates you from Christ. But you can be forgiven for your sins today." Over the next weeks and months, loads of kids made commitments to Christ in that school.

Today, forty-some years on, nothing much has changed. Sin still kills. Sin still separates us from God.

Let's be honest: True repentance, repentance that is the doorway into the blessed life, doesn't come easily to us. We're naturally self-centred people. We're going our way, and if we learn that God's way is the opposite direction, we actually don't want to turn around and truly repent. But that's not going to fly with God.

> Your iniquities have separated
> you from your God;

your sins have hidden his face from you,
     so that he will not hear.
For your hands are stained with blood,
     your fingers with guilt.
Your lips have spoken falsely,
     and your tongue mutters wicked things.
                              (Isaiah 59:2–3)

You really notice it when very sinful people get saved. People who've lived dark lives very often show it on their faces. And when these people who were deeply into depravity and addiction and all kinds of criminality meet Jesus, their whole countenance changes.

One of my friends became a Christian backstage at the Spring Harvest festival. She'd been a goth. She'd been into drug culture, pretty wild sexual depravity, and all sorts of craziness. Honestly, when she said, "Andy, I've given my life to Jesus tonight," my chin hit the floor. As I stood looking at her, her face literally changed, and I really could see a new beauty coming through.

The stain of sin screws everything up—that's why we should hate it. We've got to hate it in our own lives and our own hearts. We've got to hate its destructive effects on our world. I personally have to hate the fact that my sin nailed my Saviour to the cross. As someone has said, "It wasn't the nails that held Him there—it was my sin." He had to go through that because I'm such a wicked sinner.

But the realization of our sin shouldn't lead to self-loathing. God's discipline is designed to bring us to a positive outcome. What God wants from us out of an encounter with His holiness is that we express true repentance—the awareness of, and deep remorse for, our sins—as Isaiah did when he was cut to the quick over his unclean lips.

True repentance has been at the heart of every major move of God. We are believing for another major move of God amongst young people in our lifetime. He's promised rivers in the desert and righteousness that will shine like the noonday sun. And a sure sign of this will be repentance.

REVIVAL IS BUILT ON REPENTANCE

William Booth, the founder of the Salvation Army, signalled an incredible move of God among the least, the last, and the lost. They saw literally hundreds of thousands swept into the kingdom through bold proclamation, incredible sacrifice, and unbelievable adventures on behalf of the poor.

As it happens, my great-grandfather Captain Robert Hawthorne was one of the Salvation Army's very first missionaries to India at the end of the nineteenth century. I have become just a little bit addicted to reading about those incredible early revival days.

It is also quite remarkable how, without planning it, we at The Message seem to be re-inventing for the 21st century what the "Army" did back then. Our creative teams do the same work as their brass bands, which played the chart music of their day—in fact, the kind of music you would never hear in church. Our Eden teams and prisons work are just like the work of what the Salvation Army called The Slum Sisters and Brothers. And our businesses to provide jobs for ex-offenders are not unlike the Salvation match factories and farm colonies of those early glory days.

How exciting those days must have been. Here's a description of a Salvation Army meeting from 1879, written by a cynical journalist in the *Newcastle Daily Chronicle*:

> Until penitents "throw themselves at the feet of Jesus," as it's called, a meeting of the Salvation Army is a tolerably sane affair. The fat is at once in the fire, however, when penitents come forward.... Half a dozen crop-headed youths—boys they are, indeed—are praying vociferously, with their faces towards me. Did I say praying? I only suppose they were. It was vociferous shouting, with closed eyes. Their bodies sway to and fro; their hands are lifted, and brought down again with a thump on the form; they contort themselves as if they were in acute agony. Meanwhile the "lasses" are busy with the work of conversion.[1]

The "hallelujah lasses" were William Booth's ministry team. They tended to be ex-junkies, street women, and prostitutes, and they would minister to people as they came forward as "penitents"—those who repented of their sins and received forgiveness from God.

God, give us more penitents in schools! God, give us some penitents in prison! God, give us an army of penitents, of people who truly repent of their sins and receive real forgiveness!

This is how the reporter ends his article:

> When I reached the street and the pure air it was
> a fresh, gray morning.... "Is this the common sort
> of thing here?" I asked of the policeman outside.
> "Very," he said, "but it has reduced our charge
> sheet, and I haven't had a case for two months."[2]

That was real revival. It was built on conviction of sin and repentance. It was built on radical prayer, and the prayer meetings went on all night. It was built on amazing sacrifice, as some were even martyred in this period and the churches were trashed. But most other crime stopped and thousands were swept into the kingdom. God, give us the real thing! God, give us penitents!

'I AM ACTUALLY LOVED!'

When God showed Isaiah his sinfulness, it was actually a mercy intended for his healing. It was one of those examples of discipline that leads to life and a restored relationship with God.

Something similar happened to Ruth Devent. Her story shows that it's never too late for a broken life to be redeemed. Ruth works full-time in our Mess Café at The Message Enterprise Centre (MEC). She first came to work with us while still serving a prison sentence. Following a very dark time in her life, one of our prisons teams played a key part in Ruth's journey of transformation. From a broken life of violent abuse and addictions, now God has completely restored her. Here's Ruth's story in her own words:

Ruth Devent's Story

I was brought up in Moss Side, Manchester, in quite a dysfunctional family. My parents split up when we were very young, and for many years I was physically abused by my mum, who was an alcoholic.

When I reached my early teens, I turned to hardcore raving at the Hacienda in Manchester to escape from all of the pain. I became addicted to ecstasy and then to alcohol.

Later, when I was married with three children, the drink still had a hold on me, and I lost my husband and kids. I did get my life back on track for a while when I graduated from Manchester University with a degree in criminology in 2008. But after having another child, my life went out of control again. I ended up in an alcohol dependent relationship, which led to me going to HM Prison Styal for a wounding offence.

So I was in a really dark place. I was very angry, confused, and lost. I couldn't escape the reality of my own deep sinfulness.

But all that began to change on the morning when I met the prison chaplain. I asked her if she would pray for the victim of my offence and his family, as well as for my own family, and she did. She offered me a New Testament, which I took upstairs to my room.

The first scripture I turned to was from Matthew 11—"Come to me all who are weary ..." and I thought, "That's me. I'm so weary."

I then had an argument with God. "If You're real," I said, "prove it, because I want to rest. I'm so tired of this."

That night, He showed me my sin. I repented and said sorry for everything I'd done and asked God to forgive me if He loved me, and then I went to sleep.

The next morning, I felt really calm, and when I told all of this to the chaplain, she asked me if I gave my life to Jesus. I said I hadn't technically, but she said I actually had, and she encouraged me to continue to read my New Testament.

After that, I kept going to chapel wanting to know more. That's how I met Natalie, who was part of The Message's prisons team, and I joined their Bible study group. I had so many questions about how to have this peace and freedom. Natalie broke it down for me.

For the first eight weeks after that, I was in a single cell, and I absolutely devoured the New Testament. I stopped swearing and smoking. My whole attitude just changed. It was unbelievable because I was so angry when I first got there. I was growling at everyone. I wasn't a very nice person. I was always on the defensive, very judgemental, and I just wanted to lock myself away from everybody.

But now I didn't want to be seen as this violent, angry woman. There was a lot of hurt and fear in me. When I realised I could give it all to God, I thought, "This is amazing—I am actually loved." It changed me. I'd been completely broken, and now God was rebuilding me. I knew this was part of His plan for me because there was no other way He could've got through to me.

Officers noticed such a change that they moved me to an open unit in the prison. Then they asked me if I would like to work at The Message Enterprise Centre. Natalie worked there, and she explained that it was a café and they do a lot of work with ex-offenders. I was flabbergasted to have this opportunity. For someone to put their trust in me ... it gave me such a sense of hope.

When I was released from prison, I was amazed again, because I was offered a full-time job at the MEC. I'm still in shock, really. There are people working here who are going through what I've been through, and I have been able to support them and tell them that they need to pray and ask God for help.

It's not just a job they've given me—they've given me self-worth. I feel valued as a team member. I'm so grateful that they've given me this opportunity to show that I'm not just another statistic or another offender.

God has now restored my family life back to even better than it's ever been. I'm actually back with my husband now, after he saw such a change in me. My daughter is stunned that she's got a mum. When I left she was eight. She's eighteen now, and I've got a really good relationship with her, and she trusts me again.

This is all God's doing, and I thank Him every day.

HERE I AM. SEND ME!

"Go away from me, Lord; I am a sinful man!" (Luke 5:8b).

That's what Peter said when he'd just netted a miraculous catch of fish and suddenly realised that he was in the presence of the holy.

Again and again in Scripture, when God reveals Himself to people, they fall down flat before Him. When Moses heard the voice of God from the burning bush, he "hid his face, because he was afraid to look at God" (Exodus 3:6b). Even when God's *angel* appears to people, it is still so holy and "other" that they fall down and worship before being corrected (see Revelation 22:8–9).

The natural reaction to a confrontation with God's holiness, which we read about in chapter 2, is a person's guilt over his or her sin, which we read about in this chapter. Since we know that God's intent toward His children is always right relationship, we don't need to fear such confrontations. The guilt we feel by comparison isn't shame, as the devil gives, but an awestruck admission of God's unmatched holiness. It is a form of worship, when nothing in us dares hold place before Him and all we do is crumple and worship in tears.

As you pray for Christ's holiness to draw near to you, stand ready to find your sins exposed and brought to your mind. As you plead for Him to cleanse you (see Psalm 51:7), don't be surprised when He brings things to your mind that could make you abashed. Even things you'd forgotten. He is not doing so to shame you or cause you to shrink back from His presence. He's doing it, one, because you asked Him to! Two, because you have to take back the ground for God that you'd given to the enemy. And three, so that you will be moved down the path toward the very calling you've raised your hand to volunteer for.

From your knees—or from flat on your face—ask Him to show you what things need to be confessed, cleaned up, and made right. This may involve phone calls to people you've not spoken to for decades. This may involve you humbling yourself and admitting wrong—admitting not to God alone but also to breathing humans, which is often much harder.

God really does want a willingness to make relationships right. Sometimes, that's the hardest thing we can ever be asked to do.

But on the other side of your confession stands forgiveness and purification.

CHAPTER 3: GROUP DISCUSSION QUESTIONS

1. Discuss in your group what it makes you think when you see Christians condemning people in public. What do you think of the point made in the chapter that non-Christians are now what Christians once were, and therefore Christians have no room to condemn?

2. One day, every person will be confronted by a holy God. Work together to form a list of people your group hopes could have this confrontation here, when there's still time for them to change, rather than before the throne of judgement. Why not commit to pray for them daily?

3. How does your group respond to the statement that Christians' impact in the world is directly correlated to their own personal holiness?

4. How can Christians express holiness to and in the world without becoming sourpusses who wag their bony, judgemental fingers at everyone else?

5. Do you personally hate sin? How is that revealed in your life?

6. Agree or disagree: "The Bible talks about sin a lot, but we don't talk about it enough."

7. What area or areas of your own life do you feel God wants you to "clean up" to make you ready and qualified to hear His calling for your life?

Chapter 4

PURIFIED FOR SERVICE

Then one of the seraphim flew to me with a live coal in his hand, which he had taken with tongs from the altar. With it he touched my mouth and said, "See, this has touched your lips; your guilt is taken away and your sin atoned for."

Isaiah 6:6–7

You have been forgiven. Did you know that?

If you're a Christian, then certainly you've heard of the forgiveness that Jesus brings. It's what the cross is all about. The atoning, sin-paying, our-place-taking death of an innocent to serve as sacrifice. The Lamb of God taking away the sins of the world.

So, in one sense, you surely know you have been forgiven. All of us who have come to Christ in faith have experienced that forgiveness.

But in practical, day-to-day reality, do you believe it? Do you live like it? Or do you feel, as many do, that the sacrifice of Jesus was miraculous and wonderful and cleansed us fully … unless you sin again, especially in a big way. Because then, maybe we're coming near to being outside His favour once again. Because then, perhaps we have to do a few extra good deeds to earn our way back into the grace of God.

People who know they're forgiven can go on to tackling the big tasks of the kingdom. But if we aren't so sure of God's current, unchanging forgiveness, we can tend to think we're destined (like the dog in Proverbs 26:11) to return to our vomit. Then we're stuck dealing with the never-ending tasks of guilt-removal, shame-reduction, and self-justification. So silly and unnecessary!

When Isaiah came face to face with the blazing holiness of God, he fell on his face and knew he was undone. What other response was even possible? But God didn't come to Isaiah with the goal of crushing him or even of pointing out his sin. God's character is not to destroy but to correct and support. God brought His judgement near, not to make Isaiah writhe, but to make Isaiah pure.

An Olympic hopeful who shows up to training camp out of shape is in for some intense purification. The coach's intent, in making the candidate work out more, eat less, and do whatever else is on the programme, is not to inflict pain for pain's sake, but to bring out the potential in the athlete and to make him or her useful for the task that has been appointed.

So it was with Isaiah, and so it is with you and me. Before we can be used fully by God—and before we (or Isaiah) can actually hear the voice of God issuing the call—we need to have God do His cleansing, forgiving work in us. Our unclean lips have to be purified. We need to stand in the reality that "your guilt is taken away and your sin atoned for."

Of course, we need the guilt-removing and sin-atoning that comes with salvation. We are not God's child without receiving those. But if, after that, we don't walk in them and count them to be true for us at all times, we're His child but not a servant who hears His voice and qualifies to volunteer for His epic calling.

THE PLUNGE OF FAITH

Not long ago, my family and I were in South Africa, and both my kids, Sam and Beth, signed up to do the world's largest bridge bungee jump. It's a very, very large drop—216 metres, down into a breathtaking canyon. Michele and I, like the wimps we are, just sat and watched!

Just as Beth was getting ready to do the jump, the girl in line before her completely bottled out. Having paid £80 to get up there, she just decided she couldn't go through with it. All the staff were coaxing her, saying, "Come on, it will be amazing! You will love it!" But she was overcome with emotion. It took another 10 minutes of coaching this girl back to the edge before she finally jumped.

Beth, on the other hand, couldn't go quickly enough. It didn't matter that she'd never done a bungee jump in her life or that this was the world's largest bridge bungee. She just said, "Arrgh! Let me at it!" And I thought, "That's my girl!"

As they pulled her up afterwards, she said, "That was the best thing I've ever done in my life!"

It's a helpful picture for so many Christians. If we have to stop and wonder if Christ's forgiveness really is big enough for us, or if we suspect that it really does not continue to cover us as we commit new sin, or if we think it's possible that we can sin ourselves outside of His grace and have to earn our way back in, we're sunk. We're stuck at the front of the line, all strapped up for the jump, but having second thoughts.

No, dear friend. We have to jump. We have to leap. We have to assume, without checking how the bungees or harnesses have been fastened, that we're going to be perfectly fine. We have to cast ourselves utterly into the care of Jesus, taking Him at His word that His grace is sufficient for us, and just flinging ourselves out over the abyss.

You are all harnessed up! God's atonement and forgiveness are real, are unbreakable, and cannot be outrun or worn out. So, leap!

This means not returning to our vomit, as a dog might. This means turning from our former, destructive lifestyles, knowing that they are not our destiny. We are the ones who leap into the freedom of the Lord.

The angel purified Isaiah's lips. The Lord took away his guilt and sin. What if Isaiah had doubted this or even disputed it? He would've been stuck in his old ways and would never have had his ears opened to hear the Lord's call. Instead, he trusted that the method the Lord had employed to remove his guilt was effective, and he questioned his forgiveness no more.

You and I must stop saying, "Is God for us? Is He really? I'm not sure I'm seeing the reality of that right now." What more must God do to prove that He is for you? The living God invested everything so that you can be a man or woman of faith who partners with Him to see people won for Jesus, to see the kingdom come, and to see heaven populated.

FROM FEAR TO FAITH

Faith is a kind of immune system that filters out fears that would otherwise paralyse us. How can we worry about what's around the corner if we're remembering that, "If God is for us, who can be against us?" (Romans 8:31b).

Fear makes people do stupid things. Basing important decisions on fear is a massive mistake, yet it's one that Christians make all the time. Fear of lack leads us to make poor financial decisions. Fear of failure causes us to hold back or, worse, to sabotage our own success. Fear of being alone gets us into bad relationships.

It's a scary thing to present our plans to God and expect Him to bless them, but how often we try to do just that—especially in the area of relationships. "Yes, God, I know it's not a great idea for me to go out with someone who's not a Christian and who doesn't share my passions, but here's my plan ..." What a dangerous way to exist!

CONTAGIOUS FAITH

We all operate virally, every one of us. We're contagious people. The Message Enterprise Centre and our houses are viral environments, where faith can be "caught." But out in the world, other attitudes can be caught, as well.

What do you want to be contagious with: faith or fear? I know what I want. I want anyone who spends time with me to come away feeling like their switch has been turned on and they are ready to go again.

Hebrews 11 has worked over the years to inspire me to greater and more contagious faith. It is full of men and women of God who—because they leapt into faith—were conduits who witnessed God's power pouring out through their lives to bless the world. Abel, who was full of faith; Enoch, who walked by faith; Noah, whose family was saved by faith; Abraham, whose faith took him away from his home and made him willing to even sacrifice his son. Isaac, Jacob, Joseph, Moses, Gideon, David ... The list goes on.

Faith in God's finished work is what allows us to cast ourselves out over great chasms and know that God will be there for us.

That's not to say, though, that every leap of faith will lead to success ... or even safety.

Hebrews 11 also talks about a few whose faith got them into trouble. Jeremiah, who was beaten and imprisoned; Isaiah himself, whom we believe was ultimately sawn in half; and Zechariah, who was stoned to death. Operating by faith will not necessarily mean that everything turns out rosy. After Judas hung himself, ten out of the eleven remaining disciples were horribly martyred (John is the only one who died of old age). The way of faith is not an easy road. But it is the only road that leads to a life worth living.

Perhaps the greatest man of faith of all was the Apostle Paul. He made an incredible mark on this earth, planting churches and seeing extraordinary moves of the Spirit. In one sense, it can be said that every Christian outside of Israel (and many inside it) owes his or her salvation to that one man's faithfulness as he carried the gospel out into the wider world.

Paul counted as sure and permanent the forgiveness and atonement of Christ. His faith in his purification by God propelled him out to do the great work of Christ that he, like Isaiah, was personally called into.

Faith is contagious. Let's get infected!

LEANING INTO PURIFICATION

I love the fact that there's such a sense of destiny about the book of Isaiah. One particular phrase recurs throughout the book: "in that day". Here's a sample:

The LORD Almighty has **a day** in store
>   for all the proud and lofty,
> for all that is exalted
>   (and they will be humbled) …
> The arrogance of man will be brought low
>   and human pride humbled;
> the LORD alone will be exalted **in that day**,
>   and the idols will totally disappear.

> People will flee to caves in the rocks
>   and to holes in the ground
> from the fearful presence of the LORD
>   and the splendour of his majesty,
>   when he rises to shake the earth.
> **In that day** people will throw away
>   to the moles and bats
> their idols of silver and idols of gold,
>   which they made to worship.
>   (Isaiah 2:12, 17–20, emphasis mine)

The Day of the Lord is coming. There approaches a day when the tide will turn, a day for repentance to lead to salvation, a day for judgement to be followed by glory.

That's how I know that the renewal of the church and the transformation of society is inevitable. Why? Because the Day of the Lord is still on its way. Jesus is still Lord. He's still on the throne, and He has promised to build His church.

Guess what: I want to live in that day now! But it's only going to happen as God's people get their act together.

It's yet another reminder from Isaiah that we're not playing games here. It's serious how we live, it's serious how we pray, and it's serious how we fight sin. There's so much at stake.

So how about it? How about repenting of anything that competes in your heart for the number one slot? How about turning your back on every sin and placing Jesus in at number one, where He belongs?

Embrace God's purification. Lean into His holiness. Receive His discipline. And then leap boldly in faith in His forgiveness.

WAKE-UP CALL

What if God has called you because the time is short? What if the Lord's "Who will go for us?" question isn't some idle wish that more good things be done, and meanwhile the End Times are still millennia in the future? What if it's almost upon us?

Consider this timely bit of prophecy-come-true from the book of Isaiah:

> "See, Damascus will no longer be a city
> but will become a heap of ruins....
>
> In that day ...
> It will be as when reapers harvest the standing
> corn,
> gathering the corn in their arms—

as when someone gleans ears of corn
> in the Valley of Rephaim.
Yet some gleanings will remain,
> as when an olive tree is beaten,
leaving two or three olives on the topmost
> > branches,
> > four or five on the fruitful boughs,"
> declares the LORD,
> the God of Israel. (Isaiah 17:1, 4–6)

Seen photos of the city of Damascus lately? It's a complete tragedy. Is it literally a heap of ruins? Check. As empty as a field that has been heavily harvested? Check. Yet a few survivors picking through the rubble like gleaners in the field? Check.

I have no idea if this prophecy refers to the pile of rubble that is Damascus today. And even if it is, I have no idea if it means the Day of the Lord is finally upon us.

But it might be.

Either way, Isaiah 17 is a healthy reminder that we need to wake up when we read our Bibles. Parts of Isaiah are a bit obscure, a bit hard work. But sometimes, the prophecies inside this extraordinary book seem to collide directly with our present-day world, and this should make us seriously stop and think.

Recently, Michele and I met up with two missionary friends, wonderful people who were working in the Arab world and have come back to Manchester to plant a church among the Muslim community in the city. They've set up a stall on a local market, giving away or selling very cheaply Bibles and other Christian books in Farsi and Arabic.

They told us that the day before, they'd baptised five people, and four of them were Iranians. They commented that it feels a bit like cheating because it's so easy to lead Iranians to Jesus at the moment: "You talk to any Farsi speaker and they are just so soft to the gospel. They're jumping into the kingdom."

You might think that Iranians would be among the hardest to reach with their brutal, strict Islamic regime, but our friends told us that the system there is falling apart. "What we saw happening with the Arab Spring, what we saw in Egypt and Syria, was horrible," they said, "but it's led to an amazing opportunity for the gospel of Jesus."

But it's what they said next that really got me thinking: "With all of these events that are happening in the Middle East … we believe we're living in the very last days of planet Earth before it all comes together."

What a thought! Now, I don't know whether they're right or not. But I can tell you it sent me back to my Bible again, looking at the newspapers at what's happening and thinking hard: *Could* it be the case?

A similar thing is happening in China. After generations of mostly frustrating missionary work there, China has entered a time when, by some estimates, out of every five Chinese who are presented with the gospel, four respond in faith.

Could we be living in the most exciting generation in world history, just before Jesus returns?

If so, then it is of great urgency that we not only accept the forgiveness and purification of Christ, but we believe in it utterly and pursue holy lives. Really, who *will* go for Him in these last days?

LOOK AND BE AMAZED

One thing's for sure: lots and lots of things are going to happen in the Middle East in the days to come, because that's where all the prophecies in the Bible are focused. They—Israel and the surrounding countries—are the Bible lands. So much of what's going on in the world today is happening in the very territories where the Bible was written and where Jesus walked.

> "Look at the nations and watch—
>> and be utterly amazed.
> For I am going to do something in your days
>> that you would not believe,
>> even if you were told." (Habakkuk 1:5)

Today, the Lord says, "Look, and be amazed at what is happening around these countries in the Middle East."

Isaiah was always prophesying to three times or epochs. His message had meaning for those who heard it in his day, but it also had fulfilment in Jesus, and then it will find further meaning in the End Times. He prophesied that something was going to happen soon in

Syria, Egypt, Moab, Philistia, and the surrounding countries. Then he wrote about things that were going to happen in that same area *in a few hundred years' time* (pointing to when Jesus, the Messiah, was to come). And then, finally, he wrote about things that were going to happen *at the end of time,* also in this region. Have we finally arrived at that day?

As I've said, I love the idea that the people of God should go through life with the Bible in one hand and the newspaper (or our smartphone!) in the other, saying, "Lord, help us understand what's going on." If we felt that the return of Jesus was imminent, it would change our evangelism. It's a bit of a wake-up call, isn't it?

Somebody has got to love the gospel so much that they want to put it on a stand, that they're prepared to fight sin, that they're prepared to pray like they've never prayed before, that they're prepared to do stuff they've never done before to reach more people than they've ever reached before.

Let's be those people.

UNCLEAN LIPS ... PURIFIED

Lauren Jubb's life has been impacted in several ways by The Message. She was first reached by an Eden team, heard the gospel at a schools gig, and, most recently, graduated from The Message Academy. After winning the 2014 Urban Hero of the Year award, she announced she was applying to join an Eden team. Here's her story in her own words:

Lauren Jubb's Story

It's so important that we do whatever it takes to show young people that God loves them. If no one had taken the time to show me, I don't know where I'd be now.

I grew up in a home with a mum who was really poorly and a dad who walked out when I was seven. Even though I knew my mum loved me with all her heart, I never felt very loved—I always felt like the loose end, really rejected. By the time I was a teenager, I was angry with the world, angry with anything that came at me. I thank God for my foster parents, who were strong Christians, and the Eden Arbourthorne team, who knew exactly what I was like back then. They prayed for me and were always so supportive, sticking by me when I was an angry young girl, a real challenge to work with.

It was at an LZ7 gig where I first encountered God's love in my heart. I was 15, having loads of fun, just jumping about with my friends. When Lindz started talking about God's love for me, it really stopped me in my tracks. Because of the kind of life I'd had up to that point, I thought that either there was no God or, if there was a God, He must hate me. But in Lindz's words I heard my own story. He was describing exactly how I was feeling. I wanted what he was taking about, that love and unconditional acceptance, because I hadn't known too much of that in my own life. Up to that point, I used to feel like I was never accepted. I used to feel like I was really ugly and no one ever really liked me.

When you feel that way, and then you discover what God actually says about you, and how He loves you, and when you learn that what you've always believed is not the truth at all—that's incredible. It changes your life. I found myself saying, "I want every girl to know this. I want everyone who's ever felt that way about themselves to know the truth. They are amazing. They are created beautiful."

The Eden team were incredible. When I became a Christian and decided to follow God, they were really supportive. They helped me to understand God more and understand the Bible more. They helped me find a mentor, and they gave me so much support. They were there from day one, never giving up on me. Eden showed me a love that nothing can compare to.

When your life's been changed in that way, that's what you want to do for other people. You start to believe with all your heart that God's going to change their life too. You believe that people working alongside them are going to help change their life. God is a God of transformation. You want to scream it from the mountaintops.

So I started volunteering with the Eden team, helping out in a youth group with computer games and dance and stuff. Then I got asked to help out in a girls' group, teaching them more about the Bible and what God said about them. That was great. I knew a lot of the girls already, so it was really natural and real.

All this time, God was healing me and restoring me. I chose not to let my past overtake me, but to overtake my past.

One day, my Eden team leader told me about The Message Academy course and said I should apply for it. So I did. I think I thought I knew what Message Academy was going to be all about. I assumed it would be a year of youth work like I was used to doing in Sheffield. How wrong could I be! The first two terms in particular felt like God dealing with all the issues in me. What I've discovered is that, the more I've grown in my character, the more God's been able to use me to help others. This year has been the best I've ever had.

Message Academy has also helped me find my calling. Now I know I'm called to work with young people. It's a massive privilege to come alongside young people and talk to them about God, to get to see them open up and grow.

I've seen God move so much this year and bring some incredible transformation. On one of my placements with the Eden Bus, we met a group of three girls who were really hard work. They came right out and told us they hated us. That's really challenging when all you want to do is show them God loves them. But what I've learnt is you have to stick with it. My Eden team never gave up on me, so how could I give up on the young people I'm working with?

So we stuck it out, kept working with them and showing them we loved them. I shared my story with them, about where I've been and where I am now. One of the girls in particular could really relate to my story. By the end of the year, we saw all three of them commit their lives to Jesus.

It's amazing how God has used my personal story to impact so many lives for good. They can relate to the pain, and when I show them the way out of the pain—knowing God's love, beginning to trust in Jesus—they want to take it too.

My life is a story of transformation. My whole outlook has changed. I know I am beautiful, I'm created for a purpose, and I'm me for a reason. My relationship with my mum is so much better. I know I have a destiny. And it's all because someone did whatever it took to show me God's love.

HERE I AM. SEND ME!

How the devil wants to keep you down! How he'd love to keep you on the sidelines, where maybe you and I have spent way too long.

In military strategy, when a fighting force cannot possibly win against a superior enemy, and yet it has not yet been rounded up and destroyed, it has only one option open to it if it wishes to continue hurting the foe.

Harassment and psychological operations.

Harassment is like minor disruptions that hinder the enemy and cause him to waste his time and effort. An aggravating effect that amounts to little more than a nuisance and a general slowing or inefficiency.

Psychological operations can be much more effective. If you can convince the enemy that your own forces are far superior to what they are, and far superior to their forces, you can demoralise your foe. They will think twice about striking you. They will have to deal with deserters and fear in the ranks. They will sit back behind their lines rather than moving forward—because you have deceived them so thoroughly, despite the fact that, in reality, you have virtually no ability to oppose them.

The devil is a master of psychological warfare. He is doomed, and he knows it well. The cross and the resurrection of Christ utterly defeated him. He lies in the dust like the serpent he is, crushed beneath the heel of the Saviour.

And yet he spins his deceptions. Even now, he whispers lies that undermine our courage and strength. His strategy is in finding what doubts we have and exploiting them to the point where we no longer see ourselves—or God—accurately.

We stand inactive, hiding behind cover, when by all rights we ought to be dismantling strongholds and inheriting the land. We keep our mouths shut because he has reminded us of our own sin, and we do not speak life to those around us. Instead of making grand leaps into the will of God, we unbuckle our harness and step away from the ledge. We secretly wonder if Christ still forgives us, and our enemy makes sure to underline the heinousness of what we have done.

This goes well beyond harassment. With weapons such as these, Satan can yet win terrible victories. Oh, he is defeated; make no mistake. He is nothing but furniture—a footstool for the Lord—and a future citizen of the lake of fire. But like Saruman at the end of *The Lord of the Rings* (the books), Satan is defeated but "I fancy he could do some mischief still in a small mean way," primarily through his voice.[3]

If you are a child of God, then you are forgiven. With a permanent, titanium forgiveness that reaches beyond every horizon further than you could reach with your sin even though you had ten thousand lifetimes. This is a finished event, a dead issue. But if you do not believe this, if you accept the whisper that your lips are still unclean or you have become unclean again, despite repentance and confession, then you will never be able to serve God in the way He desires for you. Never. You will not even be able to hear His voice issuing the call.

The Lord Jesus is the ultimate "live coal" that has been used to purify your soul. The purification is done. Finished. Settled from eternity to eternity. Yes, you still sin, but confession and repentance plunge you again beneath that crimson flow that will never be exhausted.

Lean into His purification. Pursue the disciplines. Repent of known sin. Keep your eyes open for the wiles of the devil.

And then turn your mind upward, because when your lips have been purged, your ears will be opened.

CHAPTER 4: GROUP DISCUSSION QUESTIONS

1. God sent His angel to purify Isaiah's lips. Discuss with your group whether, when you came to Christ, the Lord purged your entire being in the same way. As Christians, we do still sin. But with confession and repentance, we receive His forgiveness, and we are right back to where we were before the sin. Do you believe this? Do you believe it not only for other people but also for *you*?

2. Do you believe that a person who truly loves the Lord can sin so much that it finally exceeds the Lord's atonement? The question isn't whether or not a "real" Christian would sin that much, but whether or not, if a Christian were to sin that much, he or she could finally outrun the Lord's patience or forgiveness? If so, what options would that person have?

3. Discuss with the group why you think Christians return to certain sins the way a dog returns to its vomit. How can this cycle be broken?

4. There are reports of Muslims becoming very tender-hearted toward the gospel. The same is being said for the Chinese. Perhaps you've heard similar reports from areas like Africa and South Korea and elsewhere. What would you say if someone told you he or she thought this was a strong indicator that the End Times might be upon us? Do you think the End Times are soon to begin or might still be years, centuries, or millennia away? What makes you conclude that?

5. Satan has been defeated but he's not yet been thrown into the lake of fire (see Revelation 20:10). Until then, he uses his voice and his servants to conduct a campaign of harassment and psychological warfare. He has sidelined, delayed, demoralised, and even disqualified so many of God's children through these efforts, though he has lost the war. What level of effectiveness do you feel Christendom operates at in the world today, considering his campaign? One hundred percent? Seventy-five percent? Fifty percent? Ten? What level of personal effectiveness do you feel you operate at, due to his efforts, and what needs to happen, if anything, to move toward one hundred percent?

6. The chapter asserts that our own purification and holiness are directly tied to our ability to hear the voice of God: "When your lips have been purged, your ears will be opened." Do you agree with this? Why or why not?

Chapter 5

WHAT BREAKS GOD'S HEART

*Then I heard the voice of the Lord saying, "Whom
shall I send? And who will go for us?"*

Isaiah 6:8

I don't know about you, but when I think of God Almighty, I don't think of Him as heartbroken. Or as sorrowful or morose. I think of the Lord God as mighty, triumphant, generous, loving, exuberant, and commander of all. If He wants something done, He can just do it, and nothing and no one can oppose Him. I see Him as joyful and majestic and holy. But not saddened.

Yet surely He is motivated by love, which must mean His heart can be broken. How many times in the Gospels is Jesus moved by compassion to help someone? Indeed, the entire story of the incarnation and deeds of Jesus is a mission of mercy so that those who live in darkness may see a great light and come out of their bondage. Zoom out even further, and we can say that God's heart was broken—and His love was triggered—all the way back in the Garden when His creations spurned Him and yet He provided clothing of animal skins to cover their shame and foretold that One would come to redeem them.

As soon as God had purged Isaiah's sin, Isaiah records eight of my favourite words from this whole passage: "Then I heard the voice of the Lord" (Isaiah 6:8a).

When Isaiah beheld God's holiness, his own sin was laid bare. But when God atoned for that sin, God's words were … finally … audible.

Between ourselves and the voice of God issuing a grand call to us stands our sin. It deafens us. This is a condition God will not tolerate. So He does the work we could not do for ourselves. He comes near; He bestows holiness; He gives faith; He grants repentance; He issues forgiveness—and then He speaks to us of mission and purpose!

I think I feel another Hallelujah coming on!

And what does God say? What heavenly words fall into Isaiah's newly opened ears like the first beam of sunlight falling into eyes that had been blind? He calls for someone to go out and plead for God's people to return to Him.

His heart is breaking, you see.

The message Isaiah will be asked to deliver is disturbing. It is no message of jubilation and deliverance, at least not at first. It is no message of relief or love. It is a message of judgement. Of consequences. Of discipline and of punishment. And yet it is, still, an expression of a Father's aggrieved but unending love for His stubborn, wayward, precious children.

The heart of God does break. It breaks for every sense in which this sentence remains untrue:

> Your kingdom come,
> your will be done,
> on earth as it is in heaven. (Matthew 6:10)

God's will is not done on earth in the same way and to the same degree that it is done in heaven. There are moments, surely, and there are corners of the earth, where the will of God is unleashed here. But by and large, I wonder if God looks out over humanity with the same grief with which Jesus looked out over Jerusalem:

> Jerusalem, Jerusalem, you who kill the prophets and stone those sent to you, how often I have longed to gather your children together, as a hen gathers her chicks under her wings, and you were not willing. Look, your house is left to you desolate. For I tell you, you will not see me again until you

say, "Blessed is he who comes in the name of the Lord." (Matthew 23:37–39)

As he approached Jerusalem and saw the city, he wept over it and said, "If you, even you, had only known on this day what would bring you peace—but now it is hidden from your eyes. The days will come upon you when your enemies will build an embankment against you and encircle you and hem you in on every side. They will dash you to the ground, you and the children within your walls. They will not leave one stone on another, because you did not recognise the time of God's coming to you." (Luke 19:41–44)

Yes, God's heart breaks. He could certainly snap His celestial fingers and force all things, and all people, to align with His command. But just as Jesus voluntarily limited His divinity when He came to earth as a man, God has voluntarily withheld His wrath so that men may exercise their free will to choose whether or not to follow Him.

What if God, although choosing to show his wrath and make his power known, bore with great patience the objects of his wrath—prepared for destruction? What if he did this to make the

> riches of his glory known to the objects of his
> mercy, whom he prepared in advance for glory?
> (Romans 9:22–23)

Our God has a plan, and He does not remain idle within that plan. Way back, He drew Abram to Himself and created a people of His own. He gave the Law to His people to prepare them for the Messiah. He sent Jesus to save the world; break the power of sin, death, and hell; establish the church; and send the Holy Spirit. Beginning in the Garden of Eden, God has been pursuing the remedy to His grieving heart.

One day—perhaps one day very soon—He will wrap it all up and have what He most desires.

But until then, His will is not done on earth as it is in heaven. And so He calls His servants to go out into His harvest field and to continue and extend the works of Christ across the continents and the centuries.

WHAT BREAKS THE HEART OF GOD?

If I had to sum up in one word what it is that most breaks God's heart, I would say *pain.*

Pain in its varied forms: Suffering. Hurt. Sorrow. Fear. Bondage. Oppression. Betrayal. Loss. Separation. Abuse. Hopelessness. Intimidation. Disease. Misfortune. Hate. Injustice. Depravity. Rejection. Regret. Poverty.

Jesus was quoting Isaiah when He announced what His mission on earth was going to be. See if you can detect the human pain behind each phrase below:

> He went to Nazareth, where he had been brought up, and on the Sabbath day he went into the synagogue, as was his custom. He stood up to read, and the scroll of the prophet Isaiah was handed to him. Unrolling it, he found the place where it is written:
>
> "The Spirit of the Lord is on me,
>   because he has anointed me
>   to proclaim good news to the poor.
> He has sent me to proclaim freedom for the
>   prisoners
>   and recovery of sight for the blind,
> to set the oppressed free,
>   to proclaim the year of the Lord's favour."
>
> Then he rolled up the scroll, gave it back to the attendant and sat down. The eyes of everyone in the synagogue were fastened on him. He began by saying to them, "Today this scripture is fulfilled in your hearing." (Luke 4:16–21)

The poor are suffering the pain of poverty, and so they need good news. Prisoners are suffering the pain of incarceration and other sorrows, and they need freedom. The blind are suffering the pain of not being able to see, and they need sight. The oppressed are suffering the pain of oppression, and they need freedom.

Because of the fall, Eve was cursed to give birth in pain. Because of the fall, Adam was cursed to eke out survival only through painful, backbreaking work. The fall brought pain. God's laws are for our good, for our protection. But if we break God's laws, we get hurt—and so do others.

What motivated Christ into action even through sorrow and physical exhaustion? His compassion for the masses (Matthew 14:13–14). What roused Jesus to wrath? Religious leaders hindering the people's access to God (Matthew 21:12–13; 18:6–7). What caused Him to rebuke His disciples? Well, many things! But one was when they tried to hinder children from coming to Him (Matthew 19:14). What occupied Him day and night? Bringing healing and deliverance to all who were in pain. What moved Him to weep? The death of a friend and the anguish of those left to grieve (John 11).

Pain is not natural to God's order. The universe was designed to be pain-free. God's children were never designed to live lives of suffering.

And yet here we are.

So God's heart breaks, and so He still cries today, "Whom shall I send? Who will go for us?"

Who will go out in His name and ease suffering and pain on the earth? Who will bring the year of the Lord's favour and the message of His deliverance? Who will be an ambassador of reconciliation showing the way to peace with God? Who will bring mercy and compassion and healing in His name?

Will it be you?

Yes. Yes, emphatically, yes. It will be you, if you just choose to respond.

OUR HIGH CALLING

Down the centuries of the church there have been all sorts of arguments about what the focus of the church should be. Is it front-and-centre preaching of the Word? Front-and-centre evangelism? Is it miracles that are meant to open the way to preach the gospel? Are we meant to heal the eyes of the blind as a priority? Or is it that we're meant to pour our lives into the poor and the broken, and when they see our good deeds they'll praise our Father in heaven?

Which is it? It's all of them, of course, because Jesus perfectly modelled all of them: words, works, and wonders. What a beautiful rhythm Jesus portrayed. And we see it clearly in that passage above from Luke 4, when Jesus read from the scroll of Isaiah.

What I would've given to be a fly on the wall in that synagogue that Saturday morning!

My mate bought me a ticket to a U2 concert some time ago. It cost £184. I thought, "Wow, we're going to get some good food and good entertainment, and books signed by Bono, and I'm going to get to kiss The Edge's guitar or something … something good's got to happen for £184!"

All we got was access to a bar where we had to buy our own drinks and a comfy seat with a padded cushion to watch the concert from. I mean, it was an amazing night, but perhaps not worth £184.

But how much would you pay to have been in that synagogue that morning, listening to Jesus read the Scriptures?

Just something about the way He read those Scriptures caused every eye to be fastened on Him, even before He sat down to preach His message. Normally, a synagogue message would go on a bit, and normally it would be interactive. He would say something, then people would ask questions. They'd debate and discuss. But not for Jesus. Not this time. This was the most powerful, profound sermon the world has ever heard. It was firing the starting pistols of the great gospel rescue mission: "Today this scripture is fulfilled in your hearing" (Luke 4:21b). Hundreds of years they'd been waiting since Isaiah wrote those words. And right then, these Scriptures were being fulfilled.

And that's what He did for three-and-a-half years: He preached good news to the poor, He bound up the broken-hearted, and He opened the eyes of the blind.

In Matthew 10, He invites a bunch of unschooled, ordinary, up-and-down, inconsistent guys to join in. He sends them out in His name and they start to do the same work under the anointing of the Holy Spirit. I believe that was an early glimpse of what the post-Resurrection, post-Pentecost Christian life would look like: followers of Jesus going out to do the work of Jesus, empowered by the Spirit of Jesus.

Until it all goes (seemingly) wrong. After all the prophecies were fulfilled, after three-and-a-half years of incredible ministry, it all starts to go pear-shaped. Jesus gets arrested, tried, and crucified. The disciples knew from Scripture that anyone who's nailed to a tree is cursed (Deuteronomy 21:23). They would've been forced to conclude that such a person couldn't be the Messiah.

Look closely and you'll see that this was all prophesied in the Old Testament. A thousand years before Christ—before crucifixions had even been invented—it was prophesied that the Messiah would be pierced through His hands and feet (Psalm 22:16).

But they can't see it. Even His own friends and disciples can't see it. They are so blinded by their brokenness and their fear that they have given up hope.

Until Jesus rises from the dead.

He conquers sin and death, then spends time with them convincing them He really is the fulfilment of all the prophecies and really is the Messiah. He makes breakfast for them on the beach. He teaches 500 of them in one place. He spends six weeks with them.

Then He gathers them and says, in John 20, "Boys, it's time for Me to go. I need to go back to My Father."

And the disciples respond, "No way! You're not going anywhere, Jesus. You're not leaving us again." But Jesus says, "No, it's better if I go, because if I go I can send you My Holy Spirit." And He breathes on the disciples, and He says, "Receive the Holy Spirit" (John 20:22).

From then on, the Holy Spirit wouldn't be coming and going onto individuals like He did in the Old Testament times. Neither would it be like the preview of it in Matthew 10, when He came on the disciples temporarily as they went on assignment. Now it's a permanent filling. As Jesus ascends to heaven, He arranges to send the Holy Spirit, so that now, all over the world, the Spirit is moving through anointed people who go out in the power of the Holy Spirit to spread the word of salvation and ease the pain in the world.

That same Spirit and that same mission are for us too, 2,000 years later. Because there aren't two Holy Spirits! There isn't a watered-down, "Western" kind of Holy Spirit that's a bit wet and wimpy. No, it's the same Holy Spirit that Jesus poured out on those first disciples. We're meant to move in the fullness and go out in the power of the Holy Spirit.

Don't you want more of it? Don't we need to get filled afresh and then step out in faith, speaking boldly as we preach the gospel? We're selling people short if we don't.

WHAT THE CALLING WILL CERTAINLY INVOLVE

At this point in the sequence of Isaiah 6:1–8, Isaiah has been prepared to hear the voice of God inviting him into His service. He's heard the Lord say, "Whom shall I send? And who will go for us?" Which is something he'd not been able to hear before.

These words from God give Isaiah the opportunity to volunteer. Isaiah doesn't know the content of the task to which God is calling him, and in a very real sense, he doesn't care.

That's where you have come in the sequence too. You've encountered the consuming holiness of God and have received purification and cleansing, which is what qualifies you to have access to the calling of God. He's saying to you, as well, "Whom shall I send? And who will go for us?"

In this half-second before you have the chance to say, "Here am I. Send me!" there is a moment when we can speculate about what God may have in mind for you.

Whatever it is He's going to reveal to you, should you raise your hand to volunteer, the task He's calling you to will certainly involve this one thing: *It will relieve the pain of the world.*

No doubt about it. One way or another, in a clearly connected manner or in a way more indirect, God's calling always involves the healing of the pain and the easing of the suffering endured by humans because of the fall.

When God called Abram, it was to create for Himself a people in a promised land, which advanced His plans to bring a Saviour, which advanced His ultimate plan to undo the fall and end all suffering for all time. Even God's grandest plan of all is one that erases sorrow from mankind.

When God called Moses, it was to ease the sufferings of the children of Israel in their misery under Egyptian slave masters. Note that this calling also advanced His plans to have a people in a promised land, which advanced His plans to bring a Saviour, which advanced His ultimate plan to undo the fall and end all suffering for all time.

When God called Jonah, it was to give the Ninevites the chance to turn from their sins and find faith in the only God.

> Should I not have concern for the great city of
> Nineveh, in which there are more than a hundred
> and twenty thousand people who cannot tell their
> right hand from their left? (Jonah 4:11a)

The judgement of other nations, even when their correction was not in view as it was here, had as its goal the preservation of Israel, which advanced God's plans to bring a Saviour, which advanced His ultimate plan to undo the fall and end all suffering for all time.

When God called Samuel, even as a wee lad, it was to guide His people and establish a king, which paved the way for the coming of the Saviour, a son of David, which advanced His ultimate plan to undo the fall and end all suffering for all time.

You see how it goes. When God called John the Baptist, it was to prepare the hearts of the people so they would receive the largest benefit and impact from the Saviour, who was coming to heal the broken-hearted and open the eyes of the blind and set the captives free. The coming of the Saviour accomplished many things, but chief among them were the easing of suffering and oppression on earth and the elimination of pain for eternity.

Our Lord Himself was sent and commissioned by His Father—
to achieve all the universal tasks in the cosmic drama between God
and Satan and mankind. His mission, as He Himself proclaimed
when He read that scroll from Isaiah and claimed it as His manifesto
(Luke 4:16–21), was chiefly about the alleviation of suffering on
earth and the eventual culmination of God's plan, resulting in the
alleviation of suffering forever.

Saul of Tarsus, who became the Apostle Paul, was called to take
the gospel to the world, thus directly advancing God's plan to heal
pain in the present and drive forward His eventual goal of eliminat-
ing pain for all time for those who would believe.

You can see, then, that it's no great speculation on my part to
tell you unequivocally that whatever God is going to call you to do,
it will involve the alleviation of pain here on earth and it will be a
preview of the final elimination of pain at the end of time.

When Jesus sent His disciples out to do ministry, the commission He gave them was to alleviate pain and to herald the coming of
the kingdom that would end all pain forever:

> When Jesus had called the Twelve together, he gave
> them power and authority to drive out all demons
> and to cure diseases, and he sent them out to pro-
> claim the kingdom of God and to heal those who
> were ill. (Luke 9:1–2)

To drive out demons ... because demons come only to inflict pain, destruction, misery, and death. To cure diseases and heal those who were ill ... because sickness causes suffering. To proclaim the kingdom of God ... because through it, all pain and suffering will eventually vanish.

He is still about breaking oppression, relieving suffering, binding up the broken-hearted, befriending the lonely, safeguarding the orphan and the widow and the vulnerable, fighting for the abused, welcoming the marginalised, healing the sick, elevating the humble, defending the defenceless, delivering the captive, and speaking peace to the frightened and traumatised. All of this He does here, for the suffering around us, and also with His eye firmly fixed on the joy set before us and that place where He will wipe every tear from the eyes of His people.

That's what God's always been about, and it's certainly what He's about today. No matter what He might be calling you to in your specific case, I assure you that the words of your calling will contain within them the message of these words of Jesus:

> Come to me, all you who are weary and burdened,
> and I will give you rest. Take my yoke upon you
> and learn from me, for I am gentle and humble
> in heart, and you will find rest for your souls.
> (Matthew 11:28–29)

The mission of Christ is our mission too.

Maybe we all need to do a little health check here. How are you doing in terms of preaching good news to the poor? How often do the words of life come out of your mouth? How often do you preach Jesus to your friends and neighbours and relevantly come alongside them? Not just on a stage because it's your turn to speak, or just when you go abroad on a mission trip, but how much is that the heartbeat of your life?

How much do you love the poor? How much do you bind up the broken-hearted? How often do you get involved in setting captives free? How much is that your heart? Do you long to see the broken set free, the prisoners blessed, and the most marginalised, hurting members of society healed?

How about this for a challenge: How often do you lay your hands on the sick with faith and expectancy? How often do you step out in faith to see blind eyes opened and the dead raised? Jesus said:

> As you go, proclaim this message: "The kingdom
> of heaven has come near." Heal those who are ill,
> raise the dead, cleanse those who have leprosy, drive
> out demons. Freely you have received; freely give.
> (Matthew 10:7–8)

You can do that only because Jesus said, "Receive the Holy Spirit," and, "As the Father has sent me, I am sending you" (John

20:21). As the Father sent Jesus out of the desert three-and-a-half years previously, He's now sending you.

You have a high calling. All of His children do. In fact, we need to wake up to just how high our calling is.

It may not be that we're the person to preach good news to millions like Reinhard Bonnke—but let's do it to one or two and see what happens. Maybe we're not the next Mother Teresa who's going to set up massive work in the slums of Calcutta, so we're just going to find some hurting people who live nearby and bless them. Maybe we're not going to have the next power evangelism ministry or write bestselling books, but we can lay our hands on some sick people and see what happens.

How about it? How about being someone like that?

Whatever God is going to call you to do, it will be based on the model of Jesus while He was here. It will involve the alleviation of suffering around us, and it will point toward the permanent alleviation of suffering at the end of all things. In one respect or another, His calling will be to join with the workers going out into the hurting world:

> Jesus went through all the towns and villages, teaching in their synagogues, proclaiming the good news of the kingdom and healing every disease and illness. When he saw the crowds, he had compassion on them, because they were harassed and helpless, like sheep without a shepherd. Then he

said to his disciples, "The harvest is plentiful but the workers are few. Ask the Lord of the harvest, therefore, to send out workers into his harvest field." (Matthew 9:35–38)

WHO WILL GO FOR US ... TO PRISON?

Mo's story is an amazing testimony of the power of God, who both saves and sends. Just like Isaiah, Mo had a dramatic encounter with God and could suddenly hear His voice.

God needed someone to go into a prison to reach people for Him, and as it happened, Mo was himself headed into prison for dealing drugs. Mo was transformed by the holiness of Christ, abashed by his own sin, and purified by the Lord Jesus, and then he heard God asking who would go for Him into that dark place.

Mo began to believe that God was sending him into the prisons for a purpose. During that time, he saw more than 600 men give their lives to Christ. Today, he continues to see lives transformed through his story, and he has planted a thriving church in Hull. He is also a member of my group of evangelists and himself mentors lots of young evangelists. Here is Mo's story in his own words:

Mo Timbo's Story

I was raised on a tough estate in Peckham, South London. It was a place where tensions towards the police were always simmering, and sometimes they bubbled over. Unlike many young men on the estate, I knew my father—and even respected him growing up. But as I entered my teenage years, he walked out on me and my mum.

I looked up to him, and yet at the same time I despised him. He was a lawyer, and he always encouraged me to study hard and do my homework. But he left. He wasn't physically there. Our relationship was always long-distance, over the phone, seeing me at weekends.

When I was twelve, I started hanging out with a group of men on the estate who seemed to have everything I understood as success. They had respect, the best clothes, BMWs, and nice watches and chains. My dad was ringing me to check in once a week, but these guys were there in front of me every day.

By the age of fourteen, I was selling cannabis in order to feed my own growing addiction. At just fifteen, I was stabbed five times after an altercation with a local gang—one wound missed my spine by inches. By eighteen, I was making £8,000 a month dealing crack cocaine and heroin on the south coast.

But just a year later, I was busted by undercover police. Shortly before I was picked up, I'd met a girl who would later become my wife. She'd told me all about how she was a Christian and that she had a personal relationship with Jesus. This was all meaningless to me—I was raised in the Muslim faith. But now I was heading toward prison, and I was desperate.

So I swallowed my pride and prayed: "Jesus, if You're really there, help me get out of this situation."

Not three minutes later, there was a knock on the cell door and an officer appeared. "You were supposed to go to prison tomorrow," he said. "But you're being let out until we're ready for you."

God had shown Himself, just as I'd asked. I gave myself to Him, and instantly I became so hungry for God. I had never read the Bible up to that point, but now I couldn't get enough of it. I was at every church service, helping out wherever I could. I even started preaching.

But the prison term still hung over my head. I had gotten a reprieve, and through that I had found God, but there were still consequences for the things I'd done. I began to wonder if it might actually be God's will for me to go to prison. Once that idea landed in my brain, I started to accept it. I told the Lord I would serve Him there.

From the moment I landed on the prison grounds, I knew what I was there for. I wasn't there as a gangster and a drug dealer—I was in prison as a gospel-preaching Christian! I had a literally captive audience—they couldn't go anywhere!

It was a massive mission field. I saw the Sunday chapel service grow from five men to over one hundred as rapists, murderers, and thieves were getting saved. People started coming to me with their problems, and officers would ask me to speak to certain men about issues they were facing.

Over the next eighteen months, I moved prisons three times. During that time, I had the privilege of seeing around 600 young men commit their lives to Christ as I simply shared my personal testimony and preached.

When I was at the final prison HMYOI (Her Majesty's Young Offender Institution) Thorn Cross, I met members of The Message's prisons team.

Honestly, toward the end of my sentence, my faith had begun to dry out. I'd been going and giving and preaching non-stop for months. I was encouraged to the see the results, of course, but I wasn't receiving much in the way of peer fellowship or support from mature believers. It was such a blessing, then, to have someone reach out to help me grow some roots of my own.

After I got out of prison in 2009, The Message really kicked into my life. It was a big deal adapting back to life on the outside. I married my girlfriend, Elizabeth, four weeks after I got out. You can imagine, after being locked up with a bunch of guys for eighteen months, I wasn't the best husband. I also had no job and I couldn't find one. I felt like a shadow of myself.

During this time, my church was a great support, praise God, and many of The Message guys took the time to invest in me.

The first two guys I had led to Christ in prison were from Hull, and during the next six years I'd had that city on my heart. Then in May 2015, Elizabeth and I planted a church in one of the roughest parts of Hull. We quickly grew from just the two of us to more than 130 people. We've seen many young people get saved, with thirty commitments on one Sunday alone.

I'm still involved with The Message. It was fantastic preaching and sharing my testimony at their recent Higher tour, when hundreds of young people got saved. I'm also part of a group called

Advance, led by Andy Hawthorne, in which I gather regularly with several other evangelists to sharpen our skills in sharing the gospel.

I do preach around the country, as well, but I've turned down some events because I'm pastoring a church now and I try not to be away too much. But the good thing is that, when I do leave, it gives the young evangelists I mentor the opportunity to put their skills into practice. We've seen some as young as sixteen preaching in our church.

As a dealer, I handed out something that killed people. A few years later, I'm handing out something that gives life. It's only God who does that.

HERE I AM. SEND ME!

I love the automatic contagion of events that happen when God comes near. His holiness triggers our repentance, which triggers His purification, which leads to our ears being opened to hear His call.

Where are you in this journey?

I can tell you that we sometimes get stuck if we, for whatever reason, present resistance to God's cleansing in our lives. Maybe someone hurt us and we have very good reasons for holding on to our bitterness. Maybe we don't think *that* particular sin is a very big deal. We're not responsible for our own sanctification, after all.

I'm guessing you have a real love for the Lord Jesus and His mission or you wouldn't be reading this book. So there's no judgement flowing from me to you. I struggle with releasing every sin too. And sometimes it seems that the Holy Spirit has created an unending list of them that somehow snuck into my heart.

In one sense, the purification God gives us comes in one giant event … at salvation. But in another sense, the Lord's purification is daily and ongoing. The secret isn't to become sinless somehow but to *remain in a posture of confession*, a posture of repentance and of welcoming the fresh cleansing from God.

Our ears get clogged easily, so our sequence of confession and receiving forgiveness needs to be quick, often, and without condemnation.

Okay, so look where you are now in this sequence! The hard work has been done (and is maintained in daily prayer), and now you are poised to hear the Lord asking who will go for Him into the world that is suffering a level of pain that absolutely breaks His heart.

All that is left is for you to say the thing that is already welling up inside.

CHAPTER 5: GROUP DISCUSSION QUESTIONS

1. Survey your group to learn what attitude or emotional state everyone most often thinks of God as being in. Is He primarily angry, in your mind? Is He primarily disinterested or busy with other, more important matters? Is He primarily heartbroken? Overjoyed? Frustrated? Also take a moment to examine whether there might be something in your own heart, perhaps your relationship with your earthly father, colouring why you might see God in this way.

2. In this chapter, we've looked at what breaks God's heart. What breaks *your* heart? What about the other people in your group? On the small, private scale of your own life, what has broken your heart? On a larger scale, perhaps even a global scale, what tends to bring you to tears and motivate you to want to take action?

3. If you could wave your hand and bring about the complete and permanent elimination of one major source of pain or area of suffering, what would it be?

4. How do you respond to the assertion that God's heart breaks because of human pain (and even the pain felt by creation itself; see Romans 8:22–23) and that everything He does is for the elimination or alleviation of pain, both in the world and for eternity?

5. What do you think it means that we need to wake up to just how high our calling is?

6. In light of this chapter, how likely do you think it is that God's calling on your life will be one that has you easing the suffering of those who are hurting and/or pointing people to the ultimate end of spending eternity with Christ?

Chapter 6

ACCEPTING THE CALL

And I said, "Here am I. Send me!"
Isaiah 6:8b

Now for the fun part!

I don't know if there is a more profound phrase in the Bible than this statement of Isaiah's. "Here I am, Lord. Father, I'm right here. I'm willing and able. Won't You please send me? May I please go in in Your name? I gladly ask You to give me the honour of taking Your message, whatever it is, to the world. I know Your message will be one that is designed to result in peace and joy, in reconciliation between You and mankind, and in the elimination of pain in the world. I'm here, my Lord God—won't You please let me be Your messenger?"

Can you imagine a purer expression of devotion than this? I picture the angels in heaven surrounding God's throne, with their hands constantly raised as they volunteer to be sent out on any task for the Most High. When humans achieve a similar level of adoration for the Lord, how can it but please Him a lot?

We can detect, I think, in the sequence of Isaiah 6 that God's entire intention was to send Isaiah out on a mission. To Isaiah, it may have seemed like a chance encounter with God, as a result of which he happened to overhear something God wanted done and raised his hand, jumping up and down.

But I believe God had already selected Isaiah and that He came into Isaiah's awareness with the express goal of sending him out with a life mission. The smoke in the temple, the doorposts rattling, the purification with the tongs … all of that was His way of setting Isaiah apart, giving him the vision that would propel him for forty years, and preparing him for the task.

In some ways, this passage is the pinnacle of the Old Testament. It is, I believe, on a par with Abram (Abraham) believing God's promise in Genesis 15:6 or Moses standing before Pharaoh or Noah building the ark. In the hall of fame of great biblical expressions of faith, I believe it is even on par with David standing before Goliath, the centurion's faith in Jesus' authority (Luke 7:8), Peter walking on water (Matthew 14:28–29), or Mary believing the angel's proclamation (Luke 1:38).

When you say, "Here I am. Send me!" you're giving the Lord full permission to do with you what He wills. It's glorious. It's thrilling. It's a little terrifying. And it's the greatest, and yet most natural, expression of devotion to Jesus you can make.

SAYING YES

I'm no Isaiah, but there have been some awesome moments in my life when I knew that Almighty God had spoken to me in specific ways. I have felt Him asking me the same question: "Whom shall I send? And who will go for us?" Maybe you have too.

I heard Him asking this back at the beginning of the whole Message adventure, when we embarked on launching Manchester's biggest-ever youth mission, with the promise of "rivers in the desert and streams in the wasteland."

I heard Him asking this when He was leading us to start the Eden Project and He spoke to us from Psalm 37 in a Manchester car park. He told us so clearly that, if His people would start to plant themselves in some of Britain's toughest estates, He would move and bring change and healing. And so He has.

Even more recently, God has miraculously brought Isaiah 60 to my attention through various different sources. Specifically, He has reminded me of the last sentence in the chapter, which says, "I am the LORD; in its time I will do this swiftly" (Isaiah 60:22b).

As an organisation, I believe it is fair to say that, on the back of God speaking like this, we have sought to answer Him with a cry of

"Here I am. Send me!" and tried our best to be obedient to what He was calling us to.

A DAUNTING TASK

I do, however, wonder if we would have been so keen to respond if the message we had been given was the kind of message Isaiah received in his temple encounter!

It's one thing to be given the staggering but incredible calling to bring the good news to masses of people. It's something else entirely to be asked to bring them *bad* news, even if it really is designed to bring about their good.

The Lord told Isaiah to go and warn the people of Israel that, because of their sin and rebellion, massive judgement was coming their way. That is not an easy message to carry, and I wonder what Isaiah thought when he heard it. But to his credit, his devotion did not flag, and he heartily took up this scary responsibility.

Here's what God asked Isaiah to tell Israel:

He said, "Go and tell this people:

'Be ever hearing, but never understanding;
    be ever seeing, but never perceiving.'
Make the heart of this people calloused;
    make their ears dull
    and close their eyes.

Otherwise they might see with their eyes,
> hear with their ears,
> understand with their hearts,
and turn and be healed." (Isaiah 6:9–10)

In other words, the message Isaiah was to deliver to God's people was that, because they had closed their ears to God, God was going to grant their wish and seal their ears shut. He was hardening their hearts similarly to how He did with Pharaoh in Exodus 9–11 and how He later would with the Jews with respect to faith in Jesus (Romans 11). Now, His judgement wasn't designed to destroy them but to eventually lead them back into restored relationship with Him. This was to advance His plan to bring about the Saviour and the final elimination of suffering from mankind.

I am sure you can identify with God's assessment of the nation. Our own society is equally full of sinful, self-absorbed people, and that condition is not helped by what often appears to be a largely prayerless, weak, and ineffective church.

People's hearts are hard toward God today. Evangelism is difficult. The church is often seen as boring. Christians fight with one another. The average person sees religion or relationship with God to be unimportant, and he or she has little or no interest in spiritual things.

But we know that this is not the whole story. Even in the midst of so much rebellion, sin, and selfishness, God is not passive or silent. He is still on the move. This verse is as true about Him today as it ever has been:

For the eyes of the LORD range throughout the
earth to strengthen those whose hearts are fully
committed to him. (2 Chronicles 16:9a)

God is still looking for faithful people.

In Isaiah's case, the Lord goes on to explain that Israel's behaviour and lack of obedience will lead to devastation. It's as if a legal
sentence has been passed in heaven, and it is Isaiah's task to speak the
prophecy that will put it into effect.

Is it any wonder what Isaiah's reaction to this message is: "How
long, Lord?"

Then I said, "For how long, Lord?"
And he answered:

"Until the cities lie ruined
    and without inhabitant,
until the houses are left deserted
    and the fields ruined and ravaged,
until the LORD has sent everyone far away
    and the land is utterly forsaken.
And though a tenth remains in the land,
    it will again be laid waste.
But as the terebinth and oak
    leave stumps when they are cut down,
    so the holy seed will be the stump in the
        land." (Isaiah 6:11–13)

In other words, until they've been flattened. Until Israel's confidence in its position and its false gods has been obliterated. They themselves will be decimated, which will mean great heartache and atrocity. And yet God will not forsake them utterly, and He will rebuild them into a great people.

We know that Isaiah had to keep up his role of God's prophet of gloom and doom for around forty years. He had to watch in horror as everything he prophesied came to pass.

I wonder if he ever asked God if he could maybe give a little good news—even a promise of better things to come—now and again. Perhaps it was somewhat out of God's mercy for Isaiah's tender heart that He gave him so many glimpses of the Messiah and so many prophecies that would be fulfilled at the advent of our Lord. (For starters, see Isaiah 7:14; 9:1–2; 40:3–5; and all of chapter 53.)

Finally, forty years on, Isaiah was allowed to deliver to God's people a message from the Lord that relief was coming and their discipline was at its end:

> Comfort, comfort my people,
>   says your God.
> Speak tenderly to Jerusalem,
>   and proclaim to her
> that her hard service has been completed,
>   that her sin has been paid for. (Isaiah 40:1–2a)

During those forty years, I'm sure he had to remind himself again and again of this encounter with the Lord in the temple.

When the going gets tough and the calling is hard, it's good for us to remind ourselves of why we are standing strong. In the midst of a battle season, we need to remind our souls of the times in the past when the Lord spoke to us and allow those times to fuel our gutsy persistence.

As you hear the Lord calling you into His harvest, and as you serve Him faithfully, it will not all be pleasant. You will face resistance. Obstacles and setbacks will come. People will reject the hope you want to give them. You will probably at times feel betrayed. You will be falsely accused. Friends and allies will depart. You yourself may stumble and sin, and so some of the accusations may not be false, after all!

Clearly, some sin is so serious that we can't carry on regardless, and a significant time of restoration and repentance might well be needed. But we must always keep our "Here am I. Send me!" firmly in our mind. He really did call you. You really are doing the work of the kingdom. If they opposed God Himself in this work, certainly they will oppose you.

> If you belonged to the world, it would love you as
> its own. As it is, you do not belong to the world,
> but I have chosen you out of the world. That is
> why the world hates you. Remember what I told
> you: "A servant is not greater than his master." If
> they persecuted me, they will persecute you also.
> If they obeyed my teaching, they will obey yours

also. They will treat you this way because of my
name, for they do not know the one who sent me.
(John 15:19–21)

RECOVERING OUR MISSION

Recently, I read about the incredible missionary movement at
the end of the nineteenth century. Right in my home base of
Manchester, hundreds of young men and women were laying
down their lives to take the gospel to the ends of the earth. In
one missionary meeting at Methodist Central Hall, people were
invited to volunteer to go to a dangerous part of Africa with the
good news. They were warned that the average life expectancy of
a missionary to this place was just sixteen weeks. That night, the
altar was literally crowded with young men and women willing to
lay down their lives.

On the back of this kind of amazing commitment, the evan-
gelisation of the entire world was in sight. Wave after wave of men
and women went to the far ends of the earth, heeding the call
of God to go with the message. The church of Jesus was praying,
planning, fundraising, and sending out its best to fulfil the Great
Commission.

Then, tragically, shortly after the twentieth century dawned,
mankind did an about-face. Instead of beating their swords into
ploughshares and their spears into pruning hooks, they did the
opposite. Nations took up sword against other nations, and we

entered into generations of warfare. The same Christian nations that had been sending out missionaries now turned on one another in two terrible world wars. The foot was taken off the gas pedal of world missions.

Nowadays, it's politically incorrect to say we should be trying to reach the whole world for Christ or that He really is the only Saviour and Lord. How intolerant of us! How bigoted and narrow-minded! Who do we think we are, claiming we have the only answer to all the problems of the many nations, cultures, beliefs, and orientations of the world?

We face that sort of opposition even in the church. Or else Christians seem to believe that it is a hopeless cause.

But I'm going to keep on saying it, because I know He really is our only hope. Like Isaiah, we were created to be a "going" people with a commission to take the good news from the Lord Himself to the estates of this nation and to the ends of the earth.

For more than twenty years, I've dreamt that our Eden teams—going to the nation's tough communities, often at great personal cost—could really play a part in reigniting some of this missionary fire. I'm absolutely convinced that God spoke to me at the start of the whole Eden adventure and promised that the righteousness of our cause would "shine like the noonday sun" (Psalm 37:6 NLT). "Bring it on, God!" is all I can say!

God may be calling you into the work of evangelism too (and, of course, every Christian is called to evangelism and disciple-making), or He may be calling you into another sort of ministry that would bring relief to the suffering ones. But whatever it is, keep a firm grip on what His commission to you is—because, until and unless you hear otherwise, that's still His message for you to deliver.

THE SPIRIT IS MOVING

It's not hard to feel 'on the back foot' as a Christian. Especially with the militant atheist lobby who seem to pop their heads up whenever any of us try to celebrate our Christian heritage or point out that the Christian faith really is at the heart of pretty much everything that's good about our society.

A previous Prime Minister got in hot water with a bunch of humanists for daring to state that Britain is still a Christian country, and for celebrating some of the fantastic things the church is doing up and down the land. I, for one, am glad that David Cameron wanted to say that, because he was dead right—and I'm convinced that we move away from our Christian heritage at our peril.

Perhaps, like me, David Cameron had noticed that there aren't too many secular humanist homeless shelters, orphanages, food banks, prison workers, or debt counsellors out there.

The truth, of course, is that we have no reason to feel on the back foot. The gospel has lost none of its power. It works like nothing else to change individuals' lives—and, indeed, whole communities, if we will let it.

Also, the church isn't in retreat. It is actually advancing on pretty much all fronts! Today is an exciting day in the history of the church, in fact, perhaps the most exciting day. Because almost certainly more people will come to Christ in this era than at any time since Jesus rose from the dead. All over the world, the Spirit is moving. Wouldn't it be great if we could join in the fun a bit more in Western Europe and North America?

LET'S SETTLE THIS NOW

So many people this world idolises are putting their hope in the wrong basket. Steve Jobs, for example, gave an inspirational address to college graduates just before he died. It's a brilliant speech—except it's all based in this world. He said, "I think every day, 'What would I do if I died tomorrow?' and I make sure that I've done everything I need to do in this life." How tragic to be the most brilliant businessman on earth but end up placing everything in one basket ... and then find out when you die that it's the wrong basket.

I really like Beyoncé. She's a beautiful woman and I love it when she says, "Hey, girls, you don't need to have cosmetic surgery to look beautiful. You don't need to doll yourself up. You can just be beautiful." Her whole thing is all about having a beautiful voice, a beautiful marriage, beautiful relationships. But it's all in the wrong basket, isn't it? One day, Beyoncé is going to stand before the Lord, and no amount of multimillion record sales, beautiful singing, or amazing achievements on this earth will mean diddly squat, will it?

What about the richest man on earth, Bill Gates? Here is a philanthropist who has committed to giving away pretty much all his money before he dies. What a thing! What an inspiration to other multibillionaires. Surely this is the very thing Jesus would want him to do, to give his life and his riches to counteract disease and bless the poor. But even that's not going to be enough to save him. Even giving all his $60 billion to the poor is not going to be enough to save him. Or anyone else.

I think we need to settle this in our hearts right now. If we really do believe that death will be swallowed up in victory (1 Corinthians 15:54), isn't it time we started living like it? Isn't it time to do all we can to experience the banquet and invite as many people as possible on this earth? Shouldn't we be living like there will be a glorious resurrection day for us who know Jesus? If life under the fall is cursed by pain and suffering and oppression, and we have the answer to the curse, shouldn't we be giving it out to everyone we meet?

At the end of his life, my dad's heart disease was so advanced that the hospital sent him home to die because there was nothing more they could do for him. On his very last night on earth, fighting for breath, hovering at death's door, he said to my mum, "Christine, sing for me."

My mum pulled out the *Mission Praise* hymnal and started singing all the songs she knew. She started through the alphabetical listing with "Abba Father, Let Me Be." About eight hours later, she was still singing. When she got to "Turn Your Eyes upon Jesus," Dad took his last breath.

The Lord's presence was heavy in that room. God graciously gave Mum a picture, a vision, of Dad being carried by Jesus into a beautiful garden. Ken, my dad's brother, was there. "Hey, George," he said to Dad, "wait till you see what the Lord's got prepared for you. George, it's amazing here. You won't want to go back; it's amazing!"

My mum saw my dad walk into this garden, and some of his old Christian friends who had died ahead of him were there waiting. There was a table set with aged wine and the best meat, and the presence of the Lord was there.

What a picture! What a comfort to know that. That's what we live for. That's what it's all about. And that's forever!

THE ANOINTING OF GOD

Whatever God calls you to do, it's too big for you. It's too big for me, for anyone. God hands out God-sized tasks. It's not that He wants some small thing done that humans ought to be able to handle on their own. Neither is it that He wishes to do these things on His own, though He certainly could.

Our Lord chooses to do so many of His works on earth by means of partnership with His human servants. I'm not actually sure why He does it this way. Perhaps it gives Him pleasure to build something together with His children, just as it pleases a parent to do a project with his child. Perhaps he wants the person to grow in faith as he or she sees God multiply the bread and fish, figuratively speaking, until it feeds five thousand or more. Perhaps we're being trained, tested, and fitted for our jobs in eternity.

Whatever the reason, whatever our mission, the truth is that we need God to do the things that only He can do. Unless God breaks in on these tasks and callings, and unless God chooses to display His glory and power through us, we're stuffed, aren't we?

This is what we need Him to do:

> I will go before you
> and will level the mountains;
> I will break down gates of bronze
> and cut through bars of iron.
> I will give you hidden treasures,
> riches stored in secret places,
> so that you may know that I am the LORD,
> the God of Israel, who summons you by
> name. (Isaiah 45:2–3)

There's no obstacle too great for God. If He has called us to a task, our job is to obey Him and to step forward into obedience. It's His job to level the mountains before us.

I heard a story once about the preacher of a small American church whose building was set on a mountainside and yet whose church had run out of room for its members. The pastor said, "Lord, we need You to move a mountain for us—literally. We have the faith that You can do it, but we need You to make it move." Shortly thereafter, engineers from the state knocked on the door of the church, saying the mountain they were up against was made of a type of rock they needed for road paving, and could they please dig a massive cutting out of the mountain behind the building?

That church needed God to do what only God could do. They prayed in faith, and God moved the mountain.

There's no man, no government, no scheme of hell that presents an obstacle so great that God can't flatten it in a moment. You and I can't see heroin addicts set free and families restored, not in our own strength. You and I can't, by our own power, see lifelong criminals suddenly dealing hope instead of death.

But God can. God is about mountain-levelling breakthroughs. God is the one who breaks through impossible barriers so we can step through them just as surely as when the children of Israel walked through the Red Sea on dry land.

The only way anyone can carry out a task issued by God Almighty is to do so under the anointing of God.

A DEFINITION

Now, different Christians mean different things by the term "anointing." For our purposes, I'm going to call it a divine enabling, a sort of power link to the Most High that comes into a Christian's life when he or she abides in Christ.

As you read these very familiar words of Jesus, keep in mind that the Greek word behind "remain" carries with it the sense of a deep, peaceful, not-leaving-God's-side sort of *abiding*:

> **Remain** in me, as I also **remain** in you. No branch can bear fruit by itself; it must **remain** in the vine. Neither can you bear fruit unless you **remain** in me.
>
> I am the vine; you are the branches. If you **remain** in me and I in you, you will bear much fruit; apart from me you can do nothing. If you do not **remain** in me, you are like a branch that

is thrown away and withers; such branches are picked up, thrown into the fire and burned. If you **remain** in me and my words **remain** in you, ask whatever you wish, and it will be done for you. This is to my Father's glory, that you bear much fruit, showing yourselves to be my disciples. (John 15:4–8, emphasis mine)

I don't understand how it works, but I know it's true: When I stay connected to Christ—by seeking after Him in my heart, by reading His Word, and by keeping my sins "confessed up"—there is both the power and presence of Christ in my life that is not there otherwise. When I sin and do not repent, or when I go too long without immersing myself in His Word, or when I keep quiet too long about my faith, I can actually feel that power and presence fading.

It's almost as if I'm a branch that had been plugged into the parent tree but then fell away and landed on the ground, isn't it? It's as if I'm a beautiful flower cut from the plant and placed in a vase. The water may be fresh and there may be nutrients in it, but the fact remains that my slow death has begun, even if no one can see it just yet.

I'm not talking about a loss of salvation. I'm simply saying that, when I have a daily and renewed walk with Christ, there is a power available to me—like a lamp plugged into the wall—that is simply not present when I do not have that daily and renewed walk with Christ.

That's the anointing: that power and that awareness of His presence.

When I have finished charging one of my devices and unplug it from the charger, the little blue light stays on just for a few seconds and then quickly fades to nothing. That's me when I've chosen to remain "unplugged" from Christ: I have the semblance and the after-glow of His power still, for a very brief time, but it's quickly fading and I need to get plugged back in ASAP.

If you and I have received a God-sized mission from the hand of the Lord, our only hope of accomplishing it is to have Him come through and do what only He can do … and the only way to achieve *that* is to abide in Christ and stay plugged in to the anointing power of God.

WHO WE ARE TRULY MEANT TO BE

What would happen if the church truly became what it was meant to be?

I realise that I'm a bit old to be saying this, but I really love Christian hip-hop artist Lecrae. I watched him on the biggest syndicated hip-hop show in America once, and he really stood up for Christ. During the interview, they asked him about female groupies: "Lecrae, you're making a lot of money now—number one in all the charts. How do you cope when all these girls start flinging themselves at you?"

"The way I look at it," Lecrae replied, "a car company like Nissan has to have a big marketing budget because their cars aren't that amazing. They have to advertise a lot. Whereas Ferrari hardly spends any money advertising because everyone knows they're the best, and you have to go and chase them down. That's the type of ladies I find more attractive—those who don't advertise themselves. They're so beautiful you have to chase them down."

As he was saying this, I thought, "Isn't that true of the church, as well?" If we became what we were truly meant to be, we wouldn't need to advertise—people would be chasing us down. They'd want to know: "What is going on in that place? How is it that people are getting healed, set free, delivered, growing? How are they becoming such beautiful, generous, gracious people?"

We need the anointing of God. I need it. You need it.

In the Old Testament, "the anointing" meant that the Holy Spirit came upon somebody temporarily so that, in their flesh, they could do things that fleshly people could never do. It happened to Samson, for example, and to Saul who prophesied before he became king (1 Samuel 19). That's what it means to be anointed: for God to come upon you.

Sometimes God would anoint a foreign king and motivate him to come attack Israel—to bring God's judgement. For example:

> This is what the LORD says to his anointed,
> 	to Cyrus, whose right hand I take hold of
> to subdue nations before him
> 	and to strip kings of their armour,
> to open doors before him
> 	so that gates will not be shut....
> I will strengthen you,
> 	though you have not acknowledged me,
> so that from the rising of the sun
> 	to the place of its setting

> people may know there is none besides me.
> I am the LORD, and there is no other.
>
> (Isaiah 45:1, 5b–6)

In the Old Testament, God used to come upon men like Cyrus, often at disastrous times in Israel's history, when God's people were in disarray and following after idols.

Here we are, today, in disarray too. It's crazy what's happening to our young people. More than ever, we need to be an anointed people. In the Old Testament, the anointing was limited and temporary— for a season only. But now, through the Holy Spirit indwelling every Christian, it's liberal and permanent.

We are meant to be truly anointed of God. It's something that's available to every single believer. It means you can do the things you could never do in your flesh and it means you can fulfil your God-given purpose. Because you have a purpose, something you were made for. The anointing of God enables you to fulfil the full measure of that purpose.

Do you want to be a person who, when you preach the gospel or share about Jesus, sees extraordinary things happen? When you pray for those who are broken, do you want to see God's power break in? When you lay hands on the sick, do you want more people than ever to get healed? Do you want to walk in victory?

Well, then: Remain in Him! Go after the Anointed One! Get to know Jesus! Spend time with Him! Fall in love with Jesus all over again!

GOD WILL HAVE A PEOPLE

All over the world, the Spirit is moving. I recently had the privilege of being invited to speak at the Exponential Conference in Orlando and Los Angeles, alongside many thousands of church planters from across the globe. It was so encouraging to hear what God is doing in China, in Africa, in India … There are fires of revival burning all over the world!

Do you realise that the number of Christians on planet Earth has trebled in the last hundred years? In fact, there's never been a time in history when people were becoming Christians faster. A hundred years ago, over two-thirds of the world's Christians lived in Europe. But in the last hundred years, there's been an incredible explosion in all these places that were previously so dark.

There has been an awesome move of the Spirit in my lifetime. When I was born, there wasn't any church to speak of in China. It's predicted to soon become the largest on earth. Africa was "the dark continent"—now it's an *exporter* of missionaries. Same for South Korea.

Because of all this, let me say once again that I am convinced that Jesus is coming soon. I'm not saying He's coming tomorrow (though He might!), but every day I want to be on tiptoes of expectation. I want to be saying, "God, I can see what You're doing on the earth and I want to be part of it. I will go for You! Here I am—send me! I want to have it such that, when I see You face to face, I get that 'Well done, good and faithful servant' commendation from You."

Believe me, the Lord's salvation is close at hand. I want to be part of the action wherever it's happening! I know you do too!

REJECTING HIS ADVANCES

The whole book of Isaiah is based on this theme: God will have a people, and His purposes will prevail.

Isaiah is a book of salvation and judgement, because you can't have one without the other. Nowadays, a lot of the church wants the salvation story without the judgement story. But there's no real salvation unless you're being saved from something. We're being saved from judgement because of what Christ did. God reaches out to us, determined to have a people who will share His glory and experience the blessing of being a child of God.

Did you know that the book of Isaiah contains a beautiful mirror image of the prophet's "Here am I. Send me!" statement? Here it is:

> I revealed myself to those who did not ask
> > for me;
> I was found by those who did not seek me.
> To a nation that did not call on my name,
> > I said, "Here am I, here am I." (Isaiah 65:1)

Isaiah could say "Here I am, send me" only because God had first said, "Here I am, *seek* Me." The call to seek God predates our offer to serve Him. He seeks and saves those who were lost.

God will have a people. He will populate heaven. He will have a family. He will have friends who share in His glory and work alongside Him. What a privilege!

But despite all He's done to reach out to us—ultimately, of course, by sending His own Son to die for us—if we choose to live for ourselves and reject His advances and pursue injustice and unrighteousness instead, then, after so long, God will accept our decision. It's tragic. But that's what love is like.

What if I pursue my wife, Michele, and she rejects my advances? What if she goes off with loads of other blokes, smashes up my house, and wastes all our resources? After so much of that, I'd have to say, "Despite my great love for you, Michele, we ain't got a relationship here, have we?"

Now, that is not my story, praise the Lord, but the comparison stands. After so long of God pursuing us, saying, "Here I am, here I am.... Look, here I am—I'm even willing to die for you!" if all we do is choose unrighteousness and build our own kingdoms, well, ultimately, God is going to give us our wish. He's going to leave us to it.

In that terrible day:

> My servants will eat,
>   but you will go hungry;
> my servants will drink,
>   but you will go thirsty;
> my servants will rejoice,
>   but you will be put to shame.

My servants will sing
    out of the joy of their hearts,
but you will cry out
    from anguish of heart
    and wail in brokenness of spirit.
          (Isaiah 65:13–14)

What a terrible picture of someone who's chosen to go their own way! What a stupid thing to do! It's amazing that we have the right to say no to God, but we do.

WHITE ELEPHANT

Before the Exponential Conference in Orlando, Michele and I had a few days in the Bahamas. (I know: poor us!) Down the road from where we were staying was a huge hotel complex called the Baha Mar. It was meant to be a game-changer for the Bahamas, destined to transform the country's economy. It was going to put their GDP up by 12 percent. It was a $3.5-billion-dollar development, with 2,300 bedrooms, a luxury casino, and a massive golf course designed by Jack Nicklaus. I think I'm right in saying it was the single largest development in the world at the time.

And yet the project had gone bankrupt at 97 percent complete. So instead of transforming the economy for good, it had transformed the economy for ill. There was even a threat of it bringing down the entire Bahamian economy, because businesses associated with it were going bust all over the place. It had everything there—it even had the glass in the windows—but it wasn't open for business. The golf course was finished but no one was playing. The lawyers fought over it. While we were there, people were saying, "We don't think it's ever going to open."

Thousands of people over so many years had worked so hard to build a massive white elephant. (In British parlance, a white elephant is supposed to be a gift but the cost of maintaining and owning it is so high that it actually becomes a burden to the one who receives it.)

I'm happy to report that, as of April 2018, Baha Mar had finally opened and seemed to be doing okay.

But at the time we were there, this felt like what God's talking about here in Isaiah 65. We can put all our efforts and resources into building a life that looks amazing but that is ultimately useless, empty, and bankrupt. It's possible to have it all but still be empty because we haven't turned to the Saviour.

That's the picture Isaiah paints: "Come on, people! Look at all I've got for you. Look at all you can enjoy; look at all the blessings of walking with God ... but you choose to go your own way. You choose to pursue your own agenda."

A BETTER VISION

But to those of us who have accepted His offer of relationship He says:

> See, I will create
> > new heavens and a new earth.
> The former things will not be remembered,
> > nor will they come to mind.

But be glad and rejoice for ever
    in what I will create,
for I will create Jerusalem to be a delight
    and its people a joy.
I will rejoice over Jerusalem
    and take delight in my people;
the sound of weeping and of crying
    will be heard in it no more.

Never again will there be in it
    an infant who lives but a few days,
    or an old man who does not live out his years;
the one who dies at a hundred
    will be thought a mere child;
the one who fails to reach a hundred
    will be considered accursed.
They will build houses and dwell in them;
    they will plant vineyards and eat their fruit.
        (Isaiah 65:17–21)

On earth, you see, God's judgement always has reconciliation with Him as its goal.

Do you like the sound of those verses? That's your destiny if you know Jesus. Because you've been forgiven. Because you've been accepted. Because you're walking with Him.

There is a place of no chemotherapy, no premature deaths, no stillbirths. As you read this, are you sick? Are you sad? Are you stressed? Are you broke? Here on earth, don't be surprised about that. No, this side of heaven, there are painful trials that we face.

But we've got a vision that keeps us going—a vision of a new heaven and a new earth when it's all going to be made right. It's a vision of a place we're going. Of course, we want God to break in at any moment and deliver us from life's difficulties here and now, and indeed He can. But while we wait, the vision of heaven keeps us going.

You begin to see why the African slave songs are so profound. These people were treated with appalling injustice, and yet their songs were songs of glory. "Soon and very soon, I'm going to see the king …" They had a vision, and they knew that this wasn't all there is. There is going to be a new heaven and a new earth.

Sometimes I feel like we have our eggs in the wrong basket. We expect all the blessings to be here, in this life, when actually more than 99.9 percent of the blessings are going to be *there*. They're still to come, in this new heaven and this new earth.

I think sometimes we picture heaven as a kind of upgrade of life as we know it now. But actually no, no, no. Heaven is not an upgrade—it's a totally new order of things. It's not just everything turned around—it's everything turned the right way up.

The reality is that Christians alive today will all be there, in heaven, in a hundred years' time, because we know Jesus and we've decided to say yes. We've decided to say, "Here I am, send me!" in response to Him saying "Here I am, seek Me."

WHATEVER YOU DO, FIND YOUR PLACE IN THE MISSION OF GOD

There's only one God. There's only one Lord, and we can't back down from that. He's the Way, the Truth, and the Life. Nobody gets to God except through Him. It's an offence to some, but we've got to keep the uniqueness of Christ at the centre because, even with all the anointing in the world, unless we lift high the name of Jesus, we're never going to do what we're meant to do.

Of course we love others, we operate in grace, we don't look to pick unnecessary fights—but we have to lift high the name of Jesus because Jesus is the only hope. He is the Lord! We have an inclusive gospel that's for all people, that works for every person. But no one finds their purpose outside of the exclusiveness of Christ. It's for everybody, but it's all in Him.

There's no formula for revival but there is a foundation upon which God always builds revival. Without that foundation, we're not going to see it happen. We don't know when, suddenly, God's going to do the things that He can do. The formula is God's—that's down to God. But I believe the foundation is down to us.

Here's the foundation: If we chase after Jesus, if we fight sin, if we believe in the miraculous, if we believe for the breakthrough, and if we keep Jesus central, then, when God is ready, we'll be part of the action.

My fervent prayer is to say, "Oh, God, You've given us so many promises! Please, before I die and go to be with You, will You let us see this massive harvest?" You and I need to keep going, keep chasing, keep loving, keep serving, keep praying ... because at any moment, the breakthrough could come.

MEDICAL CARE IN THE ESTATE

Laura's story is a truly inspirational one. It shows what happens when we follow God's heart and serve the poor and ease the suffering around us, and it is an amazing example of the "abundantly more" of God that we see time and time again through the Eden Project.

Laura Neilson's Story

I first encountered The Message Trust at Message 2000, when I was eighteen. I'd booked in to camp in Heaton Park with my sister and see what happened. We had decided to go because 1) Manchester sounded exciting and we had never been "up North," 2) we thought hanging out with lots of other young people would be fun, and 3) who knew if God really did do things that had been promised in the flyer? With all the prejudice and naivety of Home Counties girls, we fully expected that simply our very presence would change "the North." Oh, how I now cringe!

What actually happened that week was that God changed me and set me on a totally different life path.

I discovered a few things that week. First, that camping is essentially miserable. Second, that my DIY skills in painting a forlorn church hall in Swinton might have not been a blessing to said church. And third, that God did actually turn up. Day after day, hour after hour, God moved, and my mind was slowly blown.

At the end of the week, I walked into the Manchester Evening News Arena, and it was as if I had walked through a physical wall. And God simply said, "*Stay.* Stay in Manchester." From that moment, I did.

The next few months were surreal. I lived with some lovely students from Manchester Uni and lived off money that arrived in envelopes to my door (from where, I have no idea). When I no longer lived on the estate with the students, I returned there daily to evangelise, and more and more people turned to faith, and I saw miracles happen. I was still so naïve that I honestly thought that this is what happens when you play a guitar instead of an organ!

I joined Eden Harpurhey (the Eden Project team in the Harpurhey neighbourhood) that Christmas, living there for three years and having a great time. It was a ball to be living with a team of talented, fun, and totally faith-filled young adults. Over the three years, we tried many a tactic to bring the kingdom to Harpurhey: dance nights, kids' clubs, church services, youth clubs, trips, songs ... I look back with a massive smile on my face and giggle at some of our mishaps!

In the time I was there, God did move ... and not always in the ways we were loudly demanding of Him. Most of all, God worked in me. I started to see that life is not lived in straight lines, that opportunity is not equal, that poverty is pervasive, that darkness really does prevail in our inner cities, and that, nevertheless, hope and light and grace can break through and set people free.

After three years, I moved from Harpurhey. My wedding day was a mix of emotions as I also moved out of an area I had grown to love. My new husband and I moved to Fitton Hill in Oldham to start an Eden project and church plant with the Salvation Army. We started the same cycle of Eden again: praying for kingdom and organising the least cool youthie ever delivered under a Message banner (after realising that serving Horlicks rather than sweets improved behaviour). Meanwhile, I continued with my studies at medical school.

Over the next year, I became acutely aware that the healthcare my neighbours were actually receiving and the medicine I was learning in school did not correlate. When my neighbour had a stroke, for example, she didn't get the follow-up she needed, and her with an adult son with learning disabilities. I realised if something were to happen to her, who would look after him? My other neighbour, an alcoholic, was treated with disdain when she fell and broke her wrist. Unable to read the letter sent by the NHS, she did not go to the clinic and never had her wrist fixed, and she became permanently disabled.

Everywhere I looked, this community was being let down by health services, and the resulting health outcomes were shocking. There was suffering right around me, and I knew this broke God's heart.

A lightbulb moment came when I read a piece of academic writing by an amazing man named Julian Tudor Hart called 'The Inverse Care Law.' His research, first published in the 1970s, showed that access to healthcare varies inversely with the needs of the population. In other words, the sickest people, the neediest populations, usually get the *least* access to healthcare.

Tudor Hart was initially ostracised from the medical profession for making these claims, but his findings have been shown to be true in every country in the world, in every healthcare service. I know it because I saw it in front of my own eyes, right where I was living. I was bothered by what I saw. I was irritated in my soul. Looking back, I think that was God coming near and making me aware that He was about to do something in and through me.

Over the next few years, we campaigned with lots of other agencies in the area for the creation of a health centre right there on the estate. We were joined by the local police, the head teacher, the housing officer, and the residents. We all asked for a GP practice in Fitton Hill. Eventually the NHS said yes, that they would put in a new practice. My job, I thought, was complete.

And yet, as I walked out of the office of the NHS manager with whom I had argued about this centre for years, she gave me one last passing shot: "You could always bid to run the centre if you're so passionate." I flounced round and said, "I will."

I was being cheeky, but I think it was also my way of saying, "Here I am, Lord—send me!"

Hope Citadel Healthcare CIC was formed that day. I was still at medical school, so I was juggling school, the Eden project, and small children—and now I was Googling how to set up a community interest company and teaching myself the basics of HR and cash flow.

The vision was simple: to provide the best healthcare possible in areas of deprivation, working creatively and compassionately and never giving up on those in our care. The values were simple too: not for profit, driven by passion not by money, brimming with endless hope and compassion, always telling of grace. A fellow Eden-ite, Dr. John Patterson, was hugely supportive and helpful.

Over the last seven years, a small group of us have toiled away to deliver this dream. Some days, we get it really right. The CQC rate our practices as Outstanding, and our 20,000 patients are (mostly) grateful. Other days, it's all heartbreakingly tough. There is entrenched poverty and huge human suffering that still makes me cry and stops me in my tracks. There are constant battles for funding, buildings, and fairness and justice within the NHS.

One year at our annual doctors' study day, I spoke about Matilda, the Roald Dahl character. I love Matilda. She is clever, feisty. She sees problems and solutions. She reads people well. And she's geeky, creative, and persistent. But she also waits for the miraculous to happen.

The journey of Hope Citadel mirrors this tale. When I first joined The Message, I was not quite sure how I would fit in. I did ballet dancing instead of break-dancing! I knew more about science than any current TV shows! I had the wrong accent! I didn't know what a "ginnel" was (it's a narrow alley between buildings). On paper, I was one of the least likely people to do anything meaningful in an area of deprivation. I was essentially a scared geek. And yet, like Matilda, as my heart changed, I began to see my miraculous happen.

Nine years ago, I sat alone at a 24/7 prayer meeting. Bored and unable to pray, I started drawing. I drew a building that was a health centre called Hope in the middle of Fitton Hill with stained-glass windows at the front. I thought nothing of the picture. Just five years later, I walked into the nearly finished health centre. I had not paid much attention to the building going up as I was working lots of shifts as a junior doctor and it was all handled by the NHS architects and, being very grateful for a permanent building at all, I didn't really care what it looked like. As I walked from the back corridor into the waiting room for the first time, I was met by a double-height space, complete with stained-glass windows. It was just as I had drawn it all those years before.

I'm so glad I booked into Message 2000. I'm so glad I followed the agitation of my heart.

You, too, can follow the agitation of *your* heart. Be quietly, stubbornly determined to use all your skills to bring justice, mercy, and kingdom ... because as you walk humbly with an Almighty God, the Almighty happens.

HERE I AM. SEND ME!

You are a volunteer for God's service. Just like the host of heaven, you offer your service to Him in a purity of devotion made all the more remarkable because you are human and could choose to do otherwise. You are one whom the eyes of the Lord roam to and fro across the earth seeking. You can be one whose heart is fully His.

You don't know what God is going to ask you to do. It could be to deliver a joyous announcement of good news and great joy for all people. Or it could be to bring word of coming destruction. You know it will be about the alleviation of pain and the furtherance of God's kingdom. But the exact content of the message isn't up to you, and in your commitment to His cause, you won't mind one way or the other (most of the time!).

Because you know that God's heart is always for reconciliation and God's eyes are always on those who are in pain, and no matter how He sends you out, if it is in service of His will and plan, you will have peace in your soul.

CHAPTER 6: GROUP DISCUSSION QUESTIONS

1. What is your group's response to this statement: "When you say, 'Here I am. Send me!' you're giving the Lord full permission to do with you what He wills. It's glorious. It's thrilling. It's a little terrifying. And it's the greatest, and yet most natural, expression of devotion to Jesus you can make"?

2. Isaiah was asked to deliver "bad news" and prophecies of judgement to Israel for forty years. Talk about a time when you found yourself in the position of having to deliver bad news to someone. How did that experience feel? What helped you (or would've helped you) do it well?

3. If the calling God gives you does turn out to be something that many people will not readily receive with joy, how will you find the strength to persevere? What if you become known as a bringer of gloom and doom, if that is your calling? What if you're asked to persevere in that task for forty years or more? How do you think you would cope?

4. How would you express the idea of *anointing* as it's been defined in this chapter? What causes you to experience the power of the Spirit in your life? What causes you to experience a fading of that power? If you've ever tried to do the Lord's work though you weren't then walking in step with Him or plugged into His power, what was the result? What is your level of anointing right now, and to what do you attribute that level?

5. Describe a time in the past when you said yes to God and served Him as a willing volunteer. How did you feel when you were serving Him in that way?

6. When have you faced a situation that you know Christ called you into but in which you needed God to show up and do what only God could do? Did He come through? What happened? Did He come through but not in the way you'd expected or asked? Explain.

Chapter 7

YOUR CALLING

We've reached the point in *Here I Am* where it's appropriate to ask God to show you what He's calling you to.

You've had (or can have now, if you've not yet had) an encounter with the God of the universe, whose holiness is so intense that you knew you would, if not for His mercy, be consumed.

Like Isaiah, you have come near enough to God's righteousness to have been given a deeply sobering reminder of who He is and who you (and I) are not. Rather than harming you, however, this confrontation with holiness has set things aright in your heart. The outcome God desires when His servant meets with Him is that the sin that is there be removed so that nothing stands between the two and communion can happen.

With God's reign re-established in your heart and your sins cleared away, your ears are opened and can hear Him saying, "Whom shall I send? And who will go for us?"

And now, at long last, you're finally free to give voice to the words that I really hope have been bubbling inside you since you picked up this book. Say them with me:

Here am I. Send me!

"Here I am, Lord. You already know I'm here, of course, because the whole reason You came near and got my attention was to send me out with this mission. I've embraced Your cleansing and heard You inviting, and now, without knowing more than Your character and what Your heart breaks and beats for, I enthusiastically raise my hand to volunteer to go. I don't care what the calling will entail or if people will like it or receive it. I know that Your plans are for the immediate and ultimate removal of suffering and for the praise of Your glory, and so I say, 'Yes, I will surely go!' without needing to know more until You're ready to tell me."

IT'S BETWEEN YOU AND GOD NOW

Now there is only you standing before God in the echoing silence. You have raised your hand and shouted your glad willingness to go wherever He sends you and do whatever He instructs. And He has heard your devoted offer.

I imagine Him revelling a moment in the bliss of your volunteering. What greater joy could there be for the God of the universe than for one of His creatures, fully inside the fallen world and still beset by the flesh and wholly possessed of free will, to lay everything aside and say, "Lord, all I want is to do Your bidding. Please, let me serve You somehow"?

We sometimes wonder how we can bless God. At Christmastime, we tell children that we give gifts to one another because of what God gave us. The natural question arises: "Well, how can we give something back to God for all He's given to us?"

We give to Him by easing the suffering of those around us— by feeding the hungry and visiting the prisoner (see Matthew 25:31–46). We give to Him by being a neighbour to the one in need, though they might seem a bit "untouchable" (see Luke 10:25–37). We give our hearts to Him at salvation and in worship and in daily praise.

But I think we give God our purest gift when we set aside all our selfish goals and pleasures and offer to Him the permission to command us, sight unseen, into whatever His loving purposes might require.

Here am I, Lord. Please, please, *please* … use me. Use me up, even. Let me be part of Your plan. Let me partner with You on something. Let me relieve some infinitesimal portion of Your burden and carry some small component of Your effort. As Simon of Cyrene bore Your cross, dear Lord, won't You please grant that I carry forward the tiniest molecule of Your purpose for the world?

In the echoing silence you stand, listening for His instruction. Still your heart. Quiet your mind. Shut out the world and the beating of your heart. Open your ears to His gentle voice.

And wait.

CONFIRMING AND CLARIFYING

Wait until the calling comes. He wants you to go, so He will certainly tell you how and when and where.

Perhaps you will hear Him speak clearly and instantly. Perhaps it will take a while longer or will at first be unclear. Persist in your waiting. Make waiting an attitude of your mind. Abide in your waiting.

As you go, look around you for clarification and confirmation. Google it. Learn who is already doing similar work. Reach out to them. Encourage them. Ask them what still needs to be done. Ask where there is need. Take them to lunch and pick their brain.

Persist in prayer and in the Word. Speak to wise counsellors. Remain under the teaching of godly preachers and teachers.

You are *there*. You have reached the glorious destination, which is the beginning of the true journey. You have reached base camp and are ready to begin your ascent. God is so very proud of you. And I can't wait to find out, here or in heaven, what happened when you raised your hand to volunteer to go for God and said, "Here I am—send me!"

CONCLUSION

I think perhaps the chief lesson of Isaiah is that we must get into a place where we can hear the Lord speaking.

The Lord wants to speak; the Lord loves to speak. Yes, the Lord is constantly saying, "Here I am, seek Me," and "See, I'm doing a new thing. Do you not perceive it?" That's His part. Our part is perceiving what the Lord is saying and getting on with doing what He says.

I met a woman named Emma. She was in a queue in a shoe shop in Scotland when she felt the Lord say, "You need to speak to that girl behind the counter—I've got a word for her."

Understandably, she was a bit reluctant with it being a shoe shop. But soon, the queue faded away until it was just her and the girl. Emma plucked up the courage and said, "I think the Lord wants to say this to you ..." She didn't even know what was going to come out of her mouth, but she just prayed and forced air across her vocal chords. And out came these words: "You're going to be a great mother."

The girl looked at her in shock and then burst into tears. "How could you know that?" she asked between sobs. "No one knows. You see, I've just found out I'm pregnant. And I've booked the abortion in already! But I prayed, 'Oh, God, I feel bad about it. Even though I haven't prayed for years, please help me in this situation.' Then you come into the shop and say, 'You're going to be a great mother.'"

As Emma stood there watching, the girl went to the phone and cancelled the abortion.

Amazing. How amazing is it that we can hear Jesus, that God's heart can be poured out through us, that we can see lives changed and families restored and babies saved and salvation come, as we just walk in obedience to His voice?

God spoke to Isaiah long ago, but He speaks to His people now. Every day, in every moment, the Lord wants to be in conversation with us. Let us be open and expectant to hear the voice of the living God speaking to us.

Whatever you do, whatever you sense the Lord calling you into, you will find your place in the mission of God. We've all got a part to play. We're all on a mission because God wants to be known among the nations and because there is "a world of hurt" out there. So much pain, oppression, fear, and suffering—all of which God wants to salve and solve.

We all need to be about the great campaign of God. We all need to be ministers of reconciliation, deliverers of the oppressed, and relievers of pain. We all need to be thinking, "I'm going to reach people for Jesus. I'm going to be praying for my family. I'm going to be stepping out in faith myself. I'm going to be God's hands and feet to bring freedom and relief."

God gets great glory through ordinary people like us when we set our lives apart for His purpose, find our place in His mission, and watch transformation come in Jesus' name as a result. There is no more exciting and worthwhile life than that.

HERE I AM. SEND ME!

Andy Hawthorne's Story

Throughout this book, I've been urging you to present yourself as a response to God's calling, and I've been highlighting the stories of others who heard and obeyed God's calling. So I thought it appropriate to tell my own story, already briefly outlined in this book, of how I answered the invitation from God to be sent.

THE BEGINNINGS: MESSAGE '88 AND '89

The Message Trust has its roots in Message '88, a week-long youth mission that took place at the Manchester Apollo in 1988. The event was pioneered by me and my brother and business partner, Simon.

Having employed many young men in our Wythenshawe clothing factory and discovering how little those workers knew of Jesus, we felt stirred to do something that relevantly presented the good news in language they could understand.

I felt the vision confirmed by God when, a few hours after dreaming up the plan for what became Message '88, and feeling deflated by the scale of what we were getting into, I opened his Bible and happened to read this passage:

> Forget the former things;
>> do not dwell on the past.
> See, I am doing a new thing!
>> Now it springs up; do you not perceive it?
> I am making a way in the wilderness
>> and streams in the wasteland.
> The wild animals honour me,
>> the jackals and the owls,
> because I provide water in the wilderness
>> and streams in the wasteland,
> to give drink to my people, my chosen,
>> the people I formed for myself
>> that they may proclaim my praise.
>> (Isaiah 43:18–21)

I don't think there are actually any better or more relevant verses anywhere in the Bible that I could have read back then.

They remain the touchstone words upon which everything we do is built, and 30 years on you will see them prominently displayed around our headquarters.

Message '88 was a massive faith venture, involving the most credible bands, theatre companies, and special guests available at the time. More importantly, it was a breakthrough moment for the churches of Manchester, who got behind the project in a big way, running around 300 local missions and events in the build-up to the event and ensuring the Apollo was packed for seven nights. In all, around 20,000 young people heard the gospel message.

A repeat run at Christmas in 1989 led to us being approached by Mark Pennells, a member of one of the bands involved, about forming a full-time youth mission to schools. A new charity, Message to Schools, was the result, formed with the express purpose of taking the gospel to young people in schools through pop and dance music.

It began with a schools week in Cheadle Hulme High School in 1991 where, after a week of lessons, assemblies, and lunchtime meetings, Mark's band put on a Friday night concert in the assembly hall.

Seventy-five kids turned up, all of them looking completely bored. Mark did his music and I did my best to preach as if there were a thousand of them out there. At the end, we invited them to join Mark and me in the changing room to receive Christ. You know what? Thirty-nine spiritually hungry young people did just that! And that night, a ministry was born.

THE WORLD WIDE MESSAGE TRIBE

Message to Schools launched as a duo, with pop performances from Mark Pennells followed by gospel messages from me. But during a studio session for Mark's new material, we stumbled upon a winning formula.

We were in the studio with our producer, Zarc Porter, just throwing a few ideas around for Mark's next songs. For some reason, I started doing some jokey, gravelly style rapping. To my surprise, Mark and Zarc loved it and we quickly recorded some of this rapping on Mark's next song. Next time we were doing a gig in school, we performed it together, and the kids went mad for it. Maybe we were on to something?

We then added singers Elaine Hanley and Lorraine Williams and a rotation of dancers from local youth groups, and called ourselves The World Wide Message Tribe. It was a strange name for a band who were totally focussed on Manchester, but we liked it.

Manchester in the early 1990s was a centre of rave and dance culture, and our sound fit right in. The World Wide Message Tribe were courted by record companies as pioneers of a new credible kind of Christian dance music. We also received mainstream attention, radio play, and even chart hits, especially in the United States. Demand for the band grew and grew, yet I think it's fair to say we never abandoned what we saw as our core mission: to share the gospel in schools and serve the church in its mission.

We made a decision that the Manchester schools and churches partnership would always be our focus, and that anything else that came along, no matter how prestigious, would have to fit in with this. We also decided that any royalties we might make from the gigs and recordings would be ploughed straight back into the work. I'm convinced that these two decisions left God free to bless and open doors for the band.

Over the following years, The World Wide Message Tribe (later shortened to The Tribe) toured the United States, the UK, and Europe (all in school holidays), performing in front of well over a million young people and selling hundreds of thousands of albums.

The band/collective went through several changes of line-up before disbanding in 2004. Tribe alumni include Lindz West (now of LZ7); Cameron Dante (Bizarre, Inc.); current Message creative director Tim Owen and his wife, Emma; author and songwriter Beth Redman; and larger-than-life vocalist Deronda Lewis.

It may sound a bit much, but I do think it's fair to say that the impact of The Tribe has been felt widely, with many Christian bands and creative mission organisations crediting us with setting a standard of creative excellence and no-holds-barred gospel proclamation. New mission bands developed under the wings of The Message in Manchester include LZ7, BlushUK, Twelve24, Amongst Wolves, BrightLine, Vital Signs, and SoulBox, together with several non-musical creative teams, such as theatre company In Yer Face, dance crew Square1, and sex and relationships team Respect Me.

In addition, hundreds of young adults have been trained in creative missions through our training courses: Xcelerate, Genetik, and Message Academy.

THE EDEN NETWORK

In 1996, five years after the first Message to Schools mission week, God prompted us to start thinking more holistically about working with young people.

It started with a schools week in Benchill, Wythenshawe, at that time the most deprived neighbourhood in the UK. At a Friday night concert, over 100 local young people chose to give their lives to Christ in response to the gospel appeal. The numbers were not unusual for The Message by then. But what surprised the local church that had hosted the concert was how many of them came along to next Sunday's service—and how disruptive that would be!

That Sunday actually felt like the fulfilment of the prophecy from Isaiah 43 that was given to me years earlier.

We did our best to help the local church follow up these young people, but it became obvious that we were all ill-equipped to bring these baby Christians, with all their issues and challenges, to full maturity. Over the next few months, we saw most of them fall right back into their old, destructive lifestyles. It was absolutely gutting. There had to be a better way than this.

In hindsight, this was another "Whom shall I send? And who will go for us?" moment. God had another task for us, and the "failure" of the church to handle those new converts was the awakening that God was coming near with another set of instructions.

We began to have a vision to see Christians moving into areas like Benchill. Not just visiting there or throwing a concert, but changing addresses, packing up the sofa, and coming to live and work there, so they could support local churches in their efforts to reach young people. This bold initiative was named Eden, and the first Eden partnership was launched in 1997 in Benchill.

Thanks to a partnership with Soul Survivor (a British ministry that helps young people deepen their relationship with Jesus), a large number of enthusiastic and mostly young volunteers applied to join Eden, resulting in several new Eden projects in some of the toughest areas and estates of Manchester, including Harpurhey, Openshaw, Longsight, and the Swinton Valley in Salford. Others followed, and word quickly spread about this innovative and courageous mission adventure.

Central to Eden's ethos is the belief that in our participation in the transformation of a deprived neighbourhood, the best and most lasting change always comes from the inside out. This is how change comes in individual human life and it's how change comes to communities too.

During Eden's first decade, well over 300 people joined Eden teams, rising to over 700 by 2018. These figures make Eden one of the largest missionary-sending movements initially in the UK, but now also in South Africa, Canada, and Germany.

One of the most memorable stories of recruitment is of 73-year-old grandmother Liza Fawcett, who chose to relocate from Chorleywood, Hertfordshire (at the time, the richest council ward in England), to Harpurhey (at that time, the poorest).

Around ten years after the first Eden, God began to open doors for Eden's growth elsewhere across the country, and the Eden Network was born. Eden London was established with the goal of planting new Edens in the toughest estates of the capital, including Bow, Tollington, and Ladbroke Grove. Regional hubs then opened in Yorkshire, the North East, the Midlands, Merseyside, Wales, and Scotland, all working toward the long-term goal of 80 Eden teams in our nation's neediest neighbourhoods.

To support the early Eden teams' work and to pioneer new partnerships with churches, we converted a double-decker bus into a mobile youth centre in early 2000. Fitted out with state-of-the-art technology, games machines, and more, Eden Bus was quickly in demand across Manchester and has led to four more Eden buses up and down the country.

Getting on a bus that turned up on your doorstep is, well, as easy as getting on a bus. It can go right into the heart of the tough places with the good news.

MESSAGE 2000 AND FESTIVAL: MANCHESTER

A driving philosophy (no bus pun intended) behind the growth of The Message is that the ministry should be characterised by both social justice and unashamed gospel proclamation, embodying what Jesus called "salt", "a lamp on a stand", and "yeast" (see Matthew 5:13–16 and 13:33).

In other words, we seek to bring in the kingdom of God in both unseen ways and seen, through public gospel proclamation, through visibly serving communities by acts of kindness, and through long-term relational ministry in partnership with local churches.

I've become convinced that combining social justice with courageous proclamation of the gospel is the only way to get the job done.
One without the other is only half a gospel.

In the summer of 2000, The Message partnered with Soul
Survivor to run an ambitious city-wide youth mission, Message
2000. Around 11,000 young Christian volunteers—most of whom
took part during their summer holiday—worked in partnership with
Greater Manchester churches on social, environmental, and crime
reduction projects.

The project was hailed as a massive success, not least because,
during the ten days of work in one estate, Swinton Valley, a noto-
rious crime hot spot, there were no recorded incidences of crime.
Following the summer of 2000, police have reported a sustained
reduction in crime. Message 2000 acted as a springboard for new
Eden projects, which went on to bless these local communities for
years to come.

In the summer of 2003, The Message partnered with the Luis
Palau Evangelistic Association to put on another week-long city-wide
venture, Festival: Manchester. Over 5,000 young people got involved
in a total of 317 local community projects, many in association with
the Greater Manchester Police. Around 65,000 people from across
Manchester attended the open-air festival that took place in Heaton
Park the following weekend, featuring Luis Palau and performances
from The Tribe, Michael Tait, TobyMac, and Tim Hughes.

The model of "words and action" evangelism, which characterised Message 2000 and Festival: Manchester, inspired many similar

events across the country, including Merseyfest, NE1 in the North East, London's Soul in the City, and the nationwide Hope 08. In each case, the church led the way in bringing together local communities to deliver social action and community-building projects ranging from environmental clean-ups, painting, and car washes to barbecues, children's activities, fun days, and youth concerts.

I'm sure that these events became the catalyst for church leaders across the country to think much more seriously about community engagement. And these days, it's unusual to meet a leader who just wants to focus on their own church meetings rather than get out there and impact society.

MESSAGE IN PRISONS AND THE MESSAGE ENTERPRISE CENTRE

As The Message approached its twentieth year, God again came near and asked who would go for Him. And the Lord opened up a whole new area of ministry, once again as a practical response to an urgent need.

The Message had been working with young offenders in prisons around the North West since around 2004, following a desire to reach the most damaged and most damaging young people—those behind bars or at risk of reoffending.

The Message in Prisons Team works in prisons and young offenders' institutions across the North West, mainly with young offenders between the ages of 18 and 21. Their work spans first-contact detached work on the prison wings; Alpha, creative arts, and discipleship courses in association with prison chaplaincies; and resettlement.

The work was good, but God called me into a deeper aspect of it. Every year, hundreds of men and women were finding new life in Christ through the work. However, in too many cases, vulnerable young men and women were leaving prison with little or no support. Despite our best efforts to connect them to churches, too many new believers—who had no hope of a job and in some cases no safe place to live—were ending up back in their old criminal lifestyles.

It started to become a regular occurrence to hear of these most broken, dysfunctional, and previously thoroughly bad young people praying for their friends and leading them to Christ in their cells … who then, upon release, reverted to old patterns. It was desperate to see so many of them sent to live in totally inappropriate hostels, chaotic homes, or even the streets. Many ended up falling back into addiction and crime, and we knew God wanted something so much better for them.

That was when we became aware that God had come near again with a new set of instructions. We needed to provide these new believers with a combination of 1) a supportive, mentoring community, 2) decent housing, and 3) a way of accessing training and work, particularly for those who had fallen out of the education system at a young age. A vision was cast for a partnership between local churches, Eden teams, local housing providers, and a unique business and training hub specifically for young men and women from disadvantaged communities and those leaving custody.

After the miraculous acquisition of the 20,000-square-foot property next to The Message's HQ in Sharston, work began on developing The Message Enterprise Centre in 2012, and it was opened in January 2013 by the Chief Constable of Greater Manchester, Sir Peter Fahy. The Centre now offers training and jobs in a café, a hair and beauty salon, and property maintenance development, gardening, and landscaping businesses.

"If we can actually meet those young men and women in prison and start putting together a pathway for them [for] when they come out," says Sir Peter Fahy, "particularly through a place like this where we can start getting them into a trade, getting them to set up a small business … it's a massive opportunity for them to transform their lives and a massive saving for society in general."[4]

MESSAGE ACADEMY

Over the last thirty years, God has consistently done more than we've asked for or imagined. Why? Because the gospel is a seed, and when that seed is planted in someone's heart and in their life, it has unlimited potential for multiplication.

As the reputation of The World Wide Message Tribe and Eden grew, The Message began to receive requests from all over the country for help in establishing new projects in creative mission and community transformation. Our response was to establish a gap-year training school for young evangelists aged eighteen to twenty-five, which opened its doors in 2001. The course has evolved over the years to keep in step with the needs of each successive generation of young people. Today, it is known as Message Academy.

Students join the life of Message Academy for a full academic year, receiving Bible teaching and experiencing practical ministry while soaking up the vision and energy of a cutting-edge mission movement. To date, Message Academy has trained around fifty young adults, with many being sent into new mission initiatives across the UK and Europe and some remaining in Manchester to serve on our teams there.

Several of our key missions teams are made up of academy graduates, including all the members of BrightLine and some members of Vital Signs and Respect Me, plus our prisons and Eden teams.

MESSAGE SOUTH AFRICA, SCOTLAND, AND WALES

Around the world, others are catching our vision to grow "urban heroes" in their own unique contexts. Little by little, by God's grace, we actually are becoming a World Wide Message Tribe.

In March 2014, The Message launched its first international hub, Message South Africa. Beginning with prisons ministry around Cape Town and an Eden team in the Salt River neighbourhood, the team has a vision to expand its reach across South Africa as God opens the doors.

And in 2014 and 2015, two new UK hubs were launched to develop the three strands of our work—Creative Mission, Community Transformation, and Christ-Centred Enterprise—across the nations of Scotland and Wales. In 2016, Canada joined the family, followed by Germany in 2017.

ADVANCE 2020 AND THE PROXIMITY NETWORK

It's been wonderful to see so many new initiatives added over the last three decades. In 2017, much thought and prayer was given to the goal of seeing this kind of ministry multiplied both in the UK and globally.

As a result, two new initiatives were born in 2018. Advance 2020 is a partnership of many evangelistic ministries looking to stir up the gift of the evangelist in multiplying accountability groups. Already, hundreds of evangelists are being trained in this way. The Proximity Network is our vision to share resources and encourage people with a passion to see our most deprived communities transformed. The goal is to see long-term transformational ministry in all the UK's ten most deprived communities.

We invite others with a similar vision to join us all around the world.

HERE I AM. SEND ME!

When you sign up to be God's volunteer, it's almost always a lifetime gig. It's not a case of taking one mission and retiring. It's usually a series of missions and sub-missions that spans decades.

It's almost as if He's looking far and wide for someone to help Him with these things, and when He finds someone who is willing,

He has an unending list of tasks for that person to do. No wonder Christ urged us to pray for God to send more workers out into the harvest!

And really, who would ever want to retire from serving God like this?

VENN DIAGRAM

Use the diagram below to list your passions, your gifts, your training, your temperament, your skills, your experience, your connections, and the sorts of things God has used you to do in the past. Look for items that could go in the area where the circles overlap, things you both love to do and are gifted and/or trained to do, because those may give some insight into the sort of work God might call you to do.

THINGS I LOVE/HAVE A HEART TO DO...

THINGS I AM GIFTED TO DO...

GOD MAY BE
CALLING ME TO...

PLAY YOUR PART IN THE MESSAGE'S WORK IN THE UK AND BEYOND

PRAY

Subscribe to our regular prayer updates sent by email or by post

JOIN

Apply for Message Academy, become an urban missionary with Eden or volunteer your time

DONATE

Give a one-off gift or set up a regular gift today

Visit **message.org.uk**
to find out how you can get involved

NOTES

1.   Roberts Liardon, *God's Generals: The Revivalists* (New Kensington, PA: Whitaker House, 2008), ebook location: http://bit.ly/GodsGenerals-revivalists, accessed 26 June 2018.

2.   Liardon, *God's Generals*, ebook location: http://bit.ly/GodsGenerals-revivalists, accessed 26 June 2018.

3.   J. R. R. Tolkien, *The Return of the King* (1955), http://fnovels.com/the-return -of-the-king-page-88.html, accessed 2 July 2018.

4.   See www.message.org.uk/history/, accessed 9 August 2018.

ABOUT THE AUTHOR

Andy Hawthorne, OBE, is a British evangelist, author, and founder of The Message Trust, a Christian mission organization based in Manchester, England. His work with young people, spanning over more than twenty-five years, was initially based in Manchester but has more recently spread across the world. His gospel-focused initiatives have been particularly directed at those who are traditionally hard to reach in schools, prisons, or from disadvantaged communities. With established hub locations across the UK, The Message has also recently opened international hubs in Canada, South Africa, and Germany.

In the early days of The Message, Andy was a member of the Christian band World Wide Message Tribe, who had success in the UK and America, winning three GMA Dove Awards. He is a popular speaker at New Wine, Spring Harvest, Soul Survivor, Keswick Convention, and other Christian conferences in the UK and around the world. He is the author of several books, including *Diary of a Dangerous Vision*, *Hope Unleashed*, and *Being The Message*. He has addressed the UK and Scottish parliaments on raising aspirations amongst young people and in 2011 was awarded an OBE in the Queen's Birthday Honours list for services to young people. For the last two years he has also been awarded the UK's top charity Chief Executive at the Sunday Times Best Companies Ceremony.

Andy is married to Michele, and together they have two children, Sam and Beth.

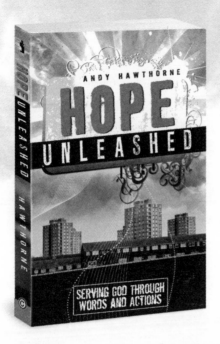

MORE FROM ANDY HAWTHORNE

Hope Unleashed challenges Christians to evangelize their communities through unashamed proclamation of the gospel and bold community action projects to reach the poor.

Committed to bringing the Christian message to youth in his hometown of Manchester, England, Andy Hawthorne was shocked when a missions partner told him he shouldn't just preach the gospel but also engage in community projects. What has washing someone's car got to do with the gospel? The idea worked, and today Hawthorne's Message Trust has been praised internationally for bringing hope and change to the roughest, poorest neighborhoods of Manchester.

Available everywhere books are sold.

DAVID C COOK

transforming lives together